Footsteps in the Snow

105 Days of lockdown

Gordon Kell

Scripture Truth Publications

Footsteps in the Snow

105 Days of lockdown

FIRST EDITION
FIRST PRINTING December 2020
ISBN: 978-0-9511515-7-0 (paperback)
Copyright © 2020 Gordon Kell and Scripture Truth Publications in this edition

Cover design by Gwyneth Duff

Published by Scripture Truth Publications
31-33 Glover Street, Crewe, Cheshire, CW1 3LD

Scripture Truth is an imprint of Central Bible Hammond Trust, a charitable trust

Typesetting by STP

This book is dedicated to the many Christians who helped me to come to faith in Christ and to grow in His grace.

And to June, my wife.

Bob,

This is the book I mentioned to you. My cousin, Eric in Hull suggested I give it to you.

Jean xx

Contents

The fruit of the Spirit

Preface

As a young man, I worked in local government for the department which had responsibility for clearing the city centre pavements of snow in the wintertime. When it snowed heavily, I had to turn up very early in the morning to help organise this work. I remember leaving my home one day after it had snowed all through the night. It was the most beautiful cloudless morning. The stars shone brightly in the dark sky, especially the North Star. An untouched carpet of deep snow covered the avenue where we lived. There was not a soul about. Most of all, I remember the exhilaration of being the first person to walk through the fresh snow to work. I didn't feel the cold. I just felt alive!

This simple experience has often reminded of me of the wonder of each day that God gives to us. We live in what can be a very dark world, but each day can be lived looking up to the One who is the Bright and Morning Star, with hope in our hearts. We can walk by faith day by day through all the experiences of life with the assurance that our times are in His hand. There is also a path which is uniquely ours. In this path, we learn the ways of God. Behind us, we leave footsteps. Some are joyful, and others are not. In front, we have yet to make footsteps. Each morning my wife, June, and I pray that the Lord would go before us guiding our steps in the ordinary and extraordinary circumstances of life.

You might be thinking footsteps in the snow quickly vanish, and you would be right in part. We are tiny, and the steps we take in life appear insignificant. But our God is a record keeper; He stores our tears in a bottle; counts the hairs on our heads; writes our names in the Lamb's Book of Life; looks for the one lost sheep; and He knows the steps we take. Our steps may disappear from our memories but not from God's because He walks in them with us.

It was while the two disciples walked home to Emmaus (Luke 24) that Jesus drew near and walked with them. That historical walk with the resurrected Christ illustrates the spiritual experience of walking with God. It is a daily experience, and I hope this small book will help you with the steps you take with the Lord.

I would like to acknowledge the tremendous help John Broadley gave in proofreading and editing the manuscript of this book. A big thank you to Gwyneth Duff for her excellent cover design and for guiding me through some technical shortcomings. I so much appreciated Richard Christian's kind and cheerful support and John Rice's kind and patient help in drawing everything together. It was a joy to work with each of them.

Introduction

"Footsteps in the Snow" was started on day three of the COVID-19 lockdown in the UK. It is a series of impressions written as I reflected on different Bible verses early each morning.

I had wanted to write a whole year series of daily Bible readings for some time, but I never expected a crisis on the scale we have passed through to be the catalyst for this book.

When lockdown began, June and I started a *WhatsApp* group called "Keep in Touch" so that Christian friends could maintain contact during the crisis. I wrote a daily post to start the day, and "Footsteps in the Snow" is a collection of the first 105 posts. As the days passed, I was encouraged by readers to consider publishing them as a book; so here we are.

Most of the content was written as stand-alone impressions, but there are also some short series based on characters and themes. The book can be used as a daily Bible reading aid or simply picked up and read in short bursts.

"Footsteps in the Snow" is intended to turn our eyes of faith to the Person who is the object of our faith: the Lord Jesus Christ. I have always believed, since becoming a Christian over 50 years ago, that the power of the Christian life comes from daily communion with the Saviour. We best follow the Lord Jesus by learning to worship Him. We become like Him by being in His presence. Central to this is allowing God to speak to us through reading the Bible and discovering Christ in its pages. If this book encourages its readers to do this, it will have served its purpose.

Day 1

Wednesday 18 March 2020

The grace of God in isolation

Rejoice in the Lord always. Again I will say, rejoice! Let your
gentleness be known to all men. The Lord is at hand. Be anxious
for nothing, but in everything by prayer and supplication, with
thanksgiving, let your requests be made known to God; and the
peace of God, which surpasses all understanding, will guard your
hearts and minds through Christ Jesus. (Philippians 4:4-7)

It is difficult to connect isolation with joy. But Paul does. He
wrote his letter to the Philippian church around twenty years
after he and Silas spent the night in the darkness of the inner
prison at Philippi. They had been beaten, their backs were sore
and bleeding, and their feet were in the stocks. They were being
punished for doing good. If ever there was a time for despair and
to doubt God, it seemed that was the time. But at midnight,
in the darkest hour, Paul and Silas prayed and sang praises to
God. The prison was filled with their joyful praise, and all the
prisoners heard them. The earthquake which followed led to the
conversion of the Philippian jailer, and that night in the jailer's
house Paul and Silas sat with their new brother in Christ. The
once hard-hearted jailor was transformed into the gentlest of
men. He expressed the reality of his salvation by the love he
showed Paul and Silas in dressing their wounds and providing
a meal, and by rejoicing with all his house. I like to think that,
as Paul's letter to the assembly at Philippi was read out, the
Philippian jailer and his family, together with Lydia and the
slave girl, sat with tears of joy rolling down their faces as they
remembered how the love of God transformed their lives. But
where was Paul writing from? He was writing from another and

longer imprisonment. Yet joy continued to fill his heart. It was a joy he wanted to share and which he speaks about in every chapter of his extraordinary letter.

It is astonishing to realise that a considerable amount of the New Testament was written from imprisonment and isolation. When darkness, and the isolation it brought, filled the land of Egypt, we read that the people of God "had light in their dwellings" (Exodus 10:23). Isolation can be lonely, but it need not be so. It can be a place where we learn the nearness of God and the joy and opportunity it brings. When Saul of Tarsus met Jesus and was blinded by His glory, he began his discipleship in the isolation of blindness with the words, "What shall I do, Lord?" That desire to serve never left him. He never viewed any circumstance he faced as confinement, even prison. They were God-given opportunities to serve and honour the Lord. Paul never ceased to ask, "What shall I do, Lord?"

In this way, Paul is an example to us to lay before God our isolation and our loneliness. We can come before God in every circumstance we face and ask the question Paul asked, "What shall I do, Lord?" In this way we can discover the will of God and the grace He gives us to accomplish it. And we shall also find the joy that comes from such a pathway. The Lord wants our experience with Him and with one another to be a joyous one: "The joy of the Lord is your strength" (Nehemiah 8:10).

Day 2

Learning to fly

> *But those who wait on the LORD*
> *Shall renew their strength;*
> *They shall mount up with wings like eagles,*
> *They shall run and not be weary,*
> *They shall walk and not faint.*
>
> *(Isaiah 40:31)*

On many occasions I have seen paragliders in Switzerland soaring above the Alps. They start by laying out their parachutes. Then they walk towards a mountain edge. Next, they run, and finally they fly. Sometimes they take one passenger with them to experience the joy of flight. It takes a lot of courage to run off the side of a mountain with a stranger!

But our Christian experience is not the same, because God works differently. To begin with, God is not a stranger, and He doesn't start from the ground, but from heaven. He takes us up into His presence to see things from where He is. Flying is the first thing we do. I remember the first time I saw a bald eagle in America soaring above the lake where we were sailing. They can see a rabbit clearly from two miles away. Coming into the presence of God to enjoy communion with Him through prayer and reading His word gives a view from heaven. This view includes the vastness of the whole counsel and the purposes of God. From this high place, God gives us the daily encouragement and guidance we need to walk with Him in all the practical details of our lives. At the end of Deuteronomy, in chapter 34, God took Moses to mount Nebo to show him the whole of the Promised Land. God can take our breath away with the scale and majesty of His counsels. But He also overwhelms us by the interest and care He has in our lives.

In God's presence we begin to understand God's greatness and God's nearness. His word provides us with clarity and focus, helping us to understand His will and the direction He wants us to take. We are empowered and inspired to run and not be tired. Spiritual energy and fruitfulness come from communion with Christ. The Lord Jesus makes this clear in John 15:5, "I am the vine, you are the branches. He who abides in Me, and I in him, bears much fruit; for without Me you can do nothing." Jesus provides all that is needed to follow and serve Him. The Lord was characterised by His service, which brought pleasure to the Father's heart. We are to be characterised by the same willingness to serve: "And whatever you do in word or deed, do all in the name of the Lord Jesus, giving thanks to God the Father through Him" (Colossians 3:17).

We are also enabled to walk and not be fatigued. Walking faithfully with God gives us the energy to serve God (see Luke 24:33). We experience a life paced by the Saviour: "Come to Me, all you who labour and are heavy laden, and I will give you rest. Take My yoke upon you and learn from Me, for I am gentle and lowly in heart, and you will find rest for your souls. For My yoke is easy and My burden is light" (Matthew 11:28-30). It is by waiting, in communion with the Father and Son by the Holy Spirit's power, that we see things from heaven, we serve with full hearts and learn to become like our Lord.

Day 3

The everlasting arms

The eternal God is your refuge,
And underneath are the everlasting arms. (Deuteronomy 33:27)

Simeon took Him up in his arms and blessed God and said:
"Lord, now You are letting Your servant depart in peace,
According to Your word;
For my eyes have seen Your salvation". (Luke 2:28-30)

It was a beautiful moment when Simeon held the Lord Jesus in his arms. It was a simple scene and, at the same time, the most profound scene. The Person who made everything lay in the arms of His old servant, just as He had lain in the manger. The theme of laying down runs throughout the life of the Lord Jesus.

The Lord Jesus lay in the manger as Immanuel. Isaiah 7:14 prophesied of the virgin bearing a child and calling His name Immanuel: "God with us". When our Queen visits the home of someone, the amount of work that goes into that visit is considerable, and its primary concern is the Queen's safety. When God stepped into creation, His primary concern was our salvation. So He came directly into the loneliness and darkness of this world. His first act was to lie down; it was to be His last act too. Jesus lay in Simeon's arms as the Saviour. Simeon said, "For my eyes have seen Your salvation". He saw in the tininess of Christ the power of redemption. Only by taking a body and becoming a man could Jesus be our Saviour. This is fundamental to our understanding of God. We cannot reach up to where He is. He comes down to where we are and in doing so brings us to Himself.

At first, it is difficult to see the Mighty God in the lowly Nazarene who, exhausted, lay down and fell asleep in the disciples' boat. But when the storm comes and the disciples fear for their lives, the Mighty God reveals Himself, and with the voice of the Creator stills the wind, sea and waves instantaneously (Mark 4:35-41). It is a marvellous illustration of how Christ lays down His life in death and rises up in all the mighty power of resurrection to lay the basis of our peace with God. There came a time when all of the prophecies, pictures and parables were fulfilled. Calvary was the place where the Lord of life laid down His life in love as the Good Shepherd. That scene of suffering, death, and sorrow was also the place where the power of the love of Christ was told out: "Therefore My Father loves Me, because I lay down My life that I may take it again. No one takes it from Me, but I lay it down of Myself. I have power to lay it down" (John 10:17-18). It was the power of love.

The Lord lay down for the last time in the grave of Joseph of Arimathea. It was from that place that He demonstrated the power of His glorious resurrection, and ensured He could place us for ever in the security and power of His everlasting arms of love. This love reminds us, in days of insecurity and uncertainty, that "underneath are the everlasting arms".

Day 4

Feeding, freeing and caring

But He put them all outside, took her by the hand and called, saying, "Little girl, arise." Then her spirit returned, and she arose immediately. And He commanded that she be given something to eat. (Luke 8:54-55)

And he who had died came out bound hand and foot with graveclothes, and his face was wrapped with a cloth. Jesus said to them, "Loose him, and let him go." (John 11:44)

But a certain Samaritan, as he journeyed, came where he was. And when he saw him, he had compassion. So he went to him and bandaged his wounds, pouring on oil and wine; and he set him on his own animal, brought him to an inn, and took care of him. On the next day, when he departed, he took out two denarii, gave them to the innkeeper, and said to him, 'Take care of him; and whatever more you spend, when I come again, I will repay you'. (Luke 10:33-35)

In the raising of Jairus' daughter, the resurrection of Lazarus and the story of the Good Samaritan, Jesus teaches us that He alone can save. But He also gives us an understanding of our spiritual responsibilities towards our family, our friends and our neighbours.

After raising Jairus' daughter, the Lord commands that she is given something to eat. This illustrates to us the importance of spiritually feeding our children in the home. In John 21 the first command of Jesus to Peter about shepherding the flock of God was to feed His lambs. The Lord especially has in mind those who are young and immature. He impresses on us the importance of ensuring they are cared for and helped in Christ.

Lazarus was a friend of Jesus – someone He loved. When He restored Lazarus to life, He commanded him to be set free from the results of death. The Lord teaches us about the power of Christian friendship. His friends had to release Lazarus from the grave clothes which prevented him from enjoying freedom of movement. We are commanded in love to help one another to be free of those things which prevent us from entering into and enjoying the liberty we have in Christ.

In the story of the Good Samaritan we have a picture of the compassionate love and care of Jesus. This is continued by the innkeeper in the light of the Samaritan's promised return. And we are left with the example to do likewise.

In our present restrictions, let us appeal to our blessed God and Father for the Lord Jesus to save. And let us minister, in humility and grace, to our families, our friends and our neighbours. All this in the certainty of His coming again.

Day 5

Sunday 22 March 2020

The Lord always looks for the isolated

Then, the same day at evening, being the first day of the week, when the doors were shut where the disciples were assembled, for fear of the Jews, Jesus came and stood in the midst, and said to them, "Peace be with you." When He had said this, He showed them His hands and His side. Then the disciples were glad when they saw the Lord. (John 20:19-20)

Isolation takes different forms. It can be felt by us personally, in our families, as the people of God, and in the world. It comes through persecution, illness, and the multitude of life's trials. This morning it is felt across the globe, separating nations, communities, generations, and families.

The Lord always looked for those who were isolated. He looked for the broken-hearted, the sick, the captives, and the lost and lonely. Thomas, one of the disciples of Jesus, was told by his fellow disciples that they had seen the Lord in resurrection. But Thomas replied, "Unless I see in His hands the print of the nails, and put my finger into the print of the nails, and put my hand into His side, I will not believe" (John 20:25).

Thomas isolated himself through wilful unbelief. But this does not stop the Lord from seeking him out. Jesus did not want Thomas to be separated from blessing. After eight days, Jesus revisited the disciples, and this time Thomas was there. The Lord immediately speaks to him, "Reach your finger here, and look at My hands; and reach your hand here, and put it into My side. Do not be unbelieving, but believing." Thomas responds to the Lord in worship, "My Lord and my God!" (John 20:27-28). He was no longer isolated.

Peter's self-confidence led him into isolation. As Jesus was led away to the High Priest's house, Peter followed at a distance. He found himself sitting amongst those who waited outside the house, and warmed himself at the fire. Three people identified him as a disciple, and three times he denied his Saviour. The cock crowed, as Jesus had foretold. It was then that Jesus, in the midst of His suffering, turned to look at Peter. His dear disciple was devastated and went out and wept bitterly. He must have felt so profoundly isolated in the bitterness of that moment. But the Lord's look was not a look of judgement. Jesus had told Peter He had prayed for Him. In the last chapter of John's Gospel, the Lord deals with Peter's self-confidence and the isolation it had taken him into. Peter's final response to the Lord's question, "Do you love Me?", was "Lord, You know all things; You know that I love You" (John 21:17). Jesus called Peter to be a shepherd and to feed His lambs and tend and feed His sheep. Later Peter would exhort elders to "Shepherd the flock of God" (1 Peter 5:2). His ministry ensured the people of God were not isolated.

The Lord Jesus taught Thomas to believe in Him and Peter to follow Him. In doing so, He ensured they were free from isolation to live in the reality of the love and grace of God. And the Lord wants this to be our experience.

Day 6

It is not for you to know

And He said to them, "It is not for you to know times or seasons which the Father has put in His own authority."   *(Acts 1:7)*

By faith Abraham obeyed when he was called to go out to the place which he would receive as an inheritance. And he went out, not knowing where he was going.   *(Hebrews 11:8)*

That I may know Him ...   *(Philippians 3:10)*

This morning we wake up in a world of uncertainty. It is a frightening place. We can be overwhelmed by not knowing what's going to happen next. As Christians, we like to be able to explain what is happening. And, like the disciples in Acts 1, we want to know what God is going to do and when He is going to do it. But Jesus gave them an answer we don't like to hear: "It is not for you to know" (Acts 1:7). It is important for us as Christians to understand that we don't know everything. Paul makes this clear at the end of 1 Corinthians 13: "For now we see in a mirror, dimly, but then face to face. Now I know in part, but then I shall know just as I also am known. And now abide faith, hope, love, these three; but the greatest of these is love" (verses 12-13).

Abraham had times when he wanted to know. He waited years for a promised son and wondered what God was doing. But Hebrews 11 records two occasions when Abraham's faith was victorious: first, in verse 8 he followed God, not knowing where he was going; later, in verses 17-18 Abraham believed God when He told him exactly where to go – the land of Moriah. God used Abraham's utter trust to foretell, through Abraham's and Isaac's experience, the death and resurrection of the Son of God.

Paul, in the five simple words "that I may know Him" (Philippians 3:10), expressed the overarching spiritual desire of his life. They remind us that it is not what we want to know but Who we need to know that is fundamentally important. Paul started his relationship with the Lord Jesus by asking who He was. The rest of his life was a journey of deepening knowledge of the Son of God, who loved him and gave Himself for him. That knowledge transformed him from a brutal, vicious man who tried to destroy the church of Christ, into the suffering, selfless, loving, and most practical saint of God who the Lord Jesus used to build His Church. He writes in Ephesians about being rooted and grounded in love and "to know the love of Christ which passes knowledge" (Ephesians 3:19).

Today, I need not be afraid of the unknown, but I need to know the One who knows all things. I need to abide in Christ and be transformed by His grace. I need to draw from Him the strength to trust Him when the way is not clear and to do the same when my pathway is clear, and always to rest in knowing the love of Christ.

Day 7

Not ceasing

Remembering without ceasing your work of faith, labour of love, and patience of hope in our Lord Jesus Christ in the sight of our God and Father. (1 Thessalonians 1:3)

For this reason we also thank God without ceasing, because when you received the word of God which you heard from us, you welcomed it not as the word of men, but as it is in truth, the word of God, which also effectively works in you who believe.

(1 Thessalonians 2:13)

Pray without ceasing. (1 Thessalonians 5:17)

Now when Daniel knew that the writing was signed, he went home. And in his upper room, with his windows open toward Jerusalem, he knelt down on his knees three times that day, and prayed and gave thanks before his God, as was his custom since early days. (Daniel 6:10)

We will remember today as the day when so much of our normal lives stopped. It is a disturbing time, filled with uncertainty. But when there is uncertainty, that's the time to reflect on things which encourage us. Paul wrote his very first letter to new believers and taught them, by example, about things which would never stop:

- He never stopped remembering the Thessalonians' faith, love and hope. It put a joy in his heart to think of all that God had done in their lives.

- He never stopped being so thankful for the Word of God that the Thessalonians had received and continued to rest upon and live by.

- He encouraged them to never stop approaching the throne of Grace in prayer and thankfulness.

Daniel had learned these things hundreds of years before (see Daniel 6). When his life was in danger, he never for a moment considered stopping praying to his God as he had done all his life. And where did he pray? In his home, which was a powerhouse of prayer. He prayed with his windows opened to Jerusalem. With a joyful hope in his heart, he knelt down in humility to pray, and with a permanent expression of thankfulness upon his lips and in his heart. This didn't stop his being cast into a den of lions, but it did stop the mouths of lions.

As we are shut up in our homes, may they not become comfortable prisons, but places of great blessing. We live in testing circumstances, but let us view them not as constraints but opportunities for our faith to be increased. We have the hope of Christ's return. This should not be a vague, distant thing, but a vivid bright star which has a present, purifying effect upon our lives. And above all may we live in the wonder of the love of God which never fails (1 Corinthians 13:8).

Day 8

The God of the universe and the God of my life

He made the stars also. *(Genesis 1:16)*

He makes me to lie down in green pastures. *(Psalm 23:2)*

I remember listening to Professor Dawkins addressing the Cambridge Union and quoting Psalm 19:1,

> "The heavens declare the glory of God;
> And the firmament shows His handiwork."

He said that was, "a god he could go for." What he could not accept was a god interested in the detail of human life.

King David wrote the words Professor Dawkins read. King David also wrote Psalm 23. David did not separate the God who "made the stars" from the God who, "made him lie down." David understood the true nature of God. He is all-powerful, all-knowing, all-seeing. But that immense power is not only displayed in the vastness and order of the universe. It is also, and more astonishingly, displayed in His care for every detail of His creation; His interest in our lives.

Jesus tells us in Matthew 10:29-30, that God knows every sparrow that falls to the ground and every hair that falls from our heads. This was not a trite saying but one which enlightens our understanding of the nature of God. People find it hard to reconcile a creator God who made the universe with a God who is interested in a tiny creature. Atheists believe in mindless forces of nature producing a universe so complex, not only in its vastness, but in the most astonishing and microscopic detail on the earth. Jesus was explaining that God is God because

He sustains the universe in its immensity and at the same time holds within His power and knowledge everything within its seen and unseen dimensions.

How is it that we as humans have a consciousness of our place in the universe and a remarkable understanding of the world we inhabit and have discovered so much about its intricacy? Why would the orderly painstaking research which emerged from our minds lead us to the conclusion that the universe is mindless? And why have people, in the words of Paul, "worshipped and served the creature rather than the Creator, who is blessed for ever. Amen" (Romans 1:25)?

Professor John Lennox once remarked that the sun is so large and so important to our earth yet it does not know I exist. But I know it exists. God made the glorious and beautiful stars but they have no relationship with Him. God made you and me, so tiny and so fragile, to have a day-by-day and eternal relationship with Him.

David looked up to the heavens and wrote of the glory of God in creation but he also looked at himself and wrote,

> "I will praise You, for I am fearfully and wonderfully made; Marvellous are Your works, And that my soul knows very well" (Psalm 139:14).

God also spoke to David of being still to know God (Psalm 46:10). These experiences led him to write "the Lord is my Shepherd" (Psalm 23:1).

Day 9

Upon His shoulders and over His heart

"And you shall put the two stones on the shoulders of the ephod as memorial stones for the sons of Israel. So Aaron shall bear their names before the Lord on his two shoulders as a memorial."

(Exodus 28:12)

"So Aaron shall bear the names of the sons of Israel on the breastplate of judgment over his heart". *(Exodus 28:29)*

He who has begun a good work in you will complete it until the day of Jesus Christ; just as it is right for me to think this of you all, because I have you in my heart. *(Philippians 1:6-7)*

I once went to a jewellery factory in Tiberias on the western shore of the Sea of Galilee. A young Jewish woman had the job of taking visitors on a short tour. The one objective of this tour was to get you into the shop to sell you some very attractive but expensive jewellery. As we walked, there were pictures of the precious stones we have read about this morning. I stopped and said to the young woman, "These are the stones which were on the breastplate of your High Priest." I will never forget the blank look on her face as the pace to the shop increased. I felt a sadness as I reflected on how little we realise how precious we are to God.

Aaron carried the people of God on his shoulders and over his heart in the presence of God. A compelling picture of the ministry of Christ, our High Priest, ever living to make intercession for us (Hebrews 7:25). Exodus 28 describes the two onyx stones set in gold on Aaron's shoulders. There was one on each of his shoulders and each stone was engraved with the names of six tribes of Israel (Exodus 28:12). I am always reminded of the Lord Jesus, describing Himself finding the lost sheep and laying it on His shoulders. There is a gentle but immense power in that action. Jesus never spoke of lifting off the sheep from His shoulders. We rest permanently in the power of Christ's salvation.

Later in Exodus 28, the breastplate Aaron wore is described as set with twelve precious stones, each engraved with the name of one of the tribes of Israel, in four rows (verses 15-21). They are mentioned three times in verses 29-30 as being on Aaron's heart. This is a great illustration of Christ's love for us which Paul describes so beautifully in Romans 8:38-39, "For I am persuaded that neither death nor life, nor angels nor principalities nor powers, nor things present nor things to come, nor height nor depth, nor any other created thing, shall be able to separate us from the love of God which is in Christ Jesus our Lord".

Day 10

Thankfulness

---

*And let the peace of God rule in your hearts, to which also you
were called in one body; and be thankful.*   *(Colossians 3:15)*

Last night we, like many others who were able to, stood outside
our homes to applaud those who work in the National Health
Service. It was a simple expression of thankfulness for the
thousands of workers who care for the increasing number of
UK citizens infected by the coronavirus. They do this work
while coping with their fears and vulnerability. They deserve
our thanks.

We do have so much to be thankful for in our lives. There are
so many material things we enjoy, not enjoyed in many parts of
the world. We have food when others go hungry, peace when
others live in war zones, freedoms when others face persecution,
order when others have chaos. We have the joys of Christian
marriage, family life, friendships, worship, fellowship and
service. Above all, we have the joy of salvation; faith, hope and
love in our Saviour, the Lord Jesus Christ; the indwelling power
of the Spirit of God, and fellowship with the Father.

Paul writes about thankfulness as something which should
characterise Christians. I am always humbled by the Saviour
when He feeds thousands of people (John 6). The Lord's eternal
glory is described in the opening verses of John 1: "All things
were made through Him, and without Him nothing was made
that was made" (verse 3). Jesus did not need the help of anyone
to feed the vast crowd before Him. But, testing Philip's faith,
Jesus asks him how they were going to feed the people. Jesus
presents it as a problem. It is then that Andrew brings the

boy with the five barley loaves and two fish. Jesus involves the disciples in getting the people sat down and ready for a meal. Then He took the loaves and gave thanks. The creator and the sustainer of the universe gave thanks to His Father in heaven for a small meal from a young boy. We should never be marked by ingratitude or unthankfulness. The Lord teaches us to be thankful. In John 12 the Lord appreciated the sacrifice Mary made when she anointed His feet with a pound of very costly oil of spikenard, and He defended her from those who criticised her action.

The Lord Jesus also gave thanks in Luke 22 when He instituted what we call the Lord's Supper. The bread and the wine represented the Lord giving His life and shedding His precious blood. Taking them, the Lord gave thanks. Paul recalls the Lord's giving of thanks in 1 Corinthians 11:24.

The Lord's thankfulness is profound and we learn from Him how to live with gratitude and appreciation in our hearts towards God, towards each other and towards all who show us kindness. Part of our witness to this world is that we are a thankful people.

Day 11

Picking up sticks

Jesus ... poured water into a basin and began to wash the disciples' feet, and to wipe them with the towel with which He was girded. (John 13:5)

Paul ... gathered a bundle of sticks and laid them on the fire ...
(Acts 28:3)

As we read John 13, we are humbled by the Lord Jesus kneeling before His disciples like a household servant to wash their feet. Before the account of this incredible act of grace, we read that Jesus knew that the Father had given all things into His hands. The majesty of His deity is magnified in His stooping. Luke records that the disciples were disputing about who should be the greatest amongst them. Even after witnessing the lowliness of the Saviour, Peter, full of self-confidence, says to the Lord Jesus, "Lord, why can I not follow You now? I will lay down my life for Your sake" (John 13:37). Against such demonstrations of the pride that so often can fill our hearts, the Lord gives us an example of the silent service of love.

In the final chapter of John's Gospel, as the disciples land the fish they had caught under the direction of the Lord, they find a fire and fish laid on it, and bread. Jesus invites them to eat breakfast, and He serves them bread and fish. Isn't it amazing that the resurrected Lord still serves His disciples?

In Acts 28 Paul and his companions were on another beach. They were rain-soaked after being shipwrecked. Everyone, as God had promised, was saved and landed, by one means and another, on Malta. I have often visualised the ageing apostle, drenched and exhausted on the beach. I have imagined his friends telling him to sit quietly and rest while they made a fire. Like the Lord Jesus, Paul did not preach or pray. Instead, he walks along the sand, gathering sticks. This was not a self-conscious act; it was the natural response of a heart that followed the Lord, a heart that had learned to serve in love.

But God responded to Paul's service in an unusual way, when a viper came out of the wood because of the heat and fastened on his hand. It was incredible that Paul had apparently carried the creature some distance, but it only fastened to his hand when everyone could see the creature bite the apostle. They expected Paul to die, but instead, he suffered no harm. Then the people changed their minds and said that he was a god. That event led him into the house of Publius, the leading citizen of the island. There Paul healed the father of Publius and began a ministry of blessing on the island, that started by collecting sticks.

When we follow the Lord and learn from Him to be gentle and lowly in heart, we are best placed to be used by Him in blessing. Paul never allowed his gift and ability to make him stand above others. He could say to the Ephesian elders, "You yourselves know that these hands have provided for my necessities, and for those who were with me" (Acts 20:34). May the Lord give us the grace to follow these examples of serving in love.

Day 12

Sunday 29 March 2020

Martha welcomes the Lord

Now it happened as they went that He entered a certain village; and a certain woman named Martha welcomed Him into her house. And she had a sister called Mary, who also sat at Jesus' feet and heard His word. But Martha was distracted with much serving, and she approached Him and said, "Lord, do You not care that my sister has left me to serve alone? Therefore tell her to help me." And Jesus answered and said to her, "Martha, Martha, you are worried and troubled about many things. But one thing is needed, and Mary has chosen that good part, which will not be taken away from her."　　　　　　　　　　　　　　(Luke 10:38-42)

I love the story of Martha. I love to read of her large-heartedness and welcoming spirit, her forthrightness, her frailties, her honesty, her faith and, of course, her service. I want to reflect on the first part of her story. In a nation where Jesus constantly faced rejection, there was one place where He was accepted – Bethany. In that town, it was Martha who welcomed Him into her home. Each Lord's Day morning, we normally travel to meet in large and small places to remember the Lord. This morning we welcome Him into our homes.

Martha wanted everything to be just right. She worked hard to feed and serve the Lord and His disciples, and became, as we well know, frustrated with the inactivity of her sister. Finally, Martha expressed her unhappiness with the situation and with the Lord.

What Jesus says to her is very interesting. He doesn't say, "Martha, you are troubled about cooking." He says, "Martha, Martha, you are worried and troubled about many things"

(Luke 10:41). Her frustration was a symptom of a burdened heart and mind. We can disguise our distress by service. We can serve others while feeling deeply burdened ourselves. Controlling and ordering every part of our lives seems to be the way to keep them on an even keel. We can fear inactivity and only see disorder when things don't go our way. This leads to dissatisfaction with others and we can be tempted to question the Lord.

The Lord Jesus knew every one of the many things which worried and troubled Martha. And He knows those things which afflict us. Jesus says in Matthew 11:28-30: "Come to Me, all you who labour and are heavy laden, and I will give you rest. Take My yoke upon you and learn from Me, for I am gentle and lowly in heart, and you will find rest for your souls. For My yoke is easy and My burden is light."

He wanted Martha, and He wants us, to learn to find peace in His presence and to understand that resting in the Lord is not inactivity but the basis of true and effective service.

One of the most difficult things to learn is to sit in the presence of the Saviour. Today we are living in a world forced to stop. May the Lord reinforce in our hearts the necessity of sitting at His feet and listening to His word. We can begin, this morning, by responding to His request to remember Him in His death and rejoice in the experience of His love, peace and power. Then go out to serve Him.

Day 13

Martha comes to Jesus

Now Jesus loved Martha and her sister and Lazarus.   (John 11:5)

Then Martha, as soon as she heard that Jesus was coming, went and met Him.   (John 11:20)

She (Martha) said to Him, "Yes, Lord, I believe that You are the Christ, the Son of God, who is to come into the world." (John 11:27)

John chapter 11 teaches us profound and powerful lessons about the ways of God. It does this within the context of a small family.

We often think of Martha as the less spiritual of two very different sisters. But this morning I want to concentrate on Martha's experience with the Lord. The background of John 11 is family sickness and death. And, right at the beginning, we read that Jesus loved Martha. It is the most powerful thing to know, amid all the testing experiences of life, that the love of Christ is consistent. I cannot explain the suffering so many families have to face. We, as a family, cannot explain nor do we understand why my father died in a hit and run accident, why June's beloved brother committed suicide, or why our daughter's happy Christian marriage ended in divorce. But we have come to understand, in all the frailty of our faith, the reality of the love of Christ. Martha may have been weaker in faith than other believers. But she is placed first when Jesus' love is recorded. The Lord always puts the weakest first.

When the Lord arrived in Bethany, Martha instinctively went to meet Him. In our need, there is no better place to be than in the presence of the Lord. He asks us to come to Him. In the

Old Testament, Esther feared to approach her husband, King Ahasuerus, uninvited. Her safety depended upon him stretching out his golden sceptre (Esther 5:2). We are to approach the throne of grace boldly. The Lord's sceptre is never withdrawn.

The Lord used Martha's meeting with Him to reveal to her and to us that He is the resurrection and the life. It is in coming to Him that we learn the deep things of Christ.

The Lord asked Martha if she believed. We like to recall Peter declaring to the Lord Jesus, "You are the Christ, the Son of the living God" (Matthew 16:16). We don't often reflect on Martha's response, "Yes, Lord, I believe that You are the Christ, the Son of God, who is to come into the world" (John 11:27). Like Peter, her faith would still stumble, but I believe it was a joy to the Lord's heart to hear her words and to lead her into a closer relationship with Himself. Our faith may be weak; our Saviour is not.

Day 14

Tuesday 31 March 2020

Martha is encouraged to believe

"Did I not say to you that if you would believe you would see the glory of God?" (John 11:40)

We closed yesterday with Martha's response to Jesus, "Yes, Lord, I believe that You are the Christ, the Son of God, who is to come into the world" (John 11:27). Martha's heart for the Lord was unquestioned. And, as we have seen, she is characterised by activity, openness and frankness. The Lord uses her experiences with Him to teach lessons we need to learn.

But Martha surprises us too. The discretion she demonstrates as she quietly tells her sister the Lord was calling her is appealing. There was tenderness at that moment which showed her care for her grieving sister. Martha was a strong woman at the centre of a family she cared for and wanted to protect at a time of loss. When Mary, the people and the Lord wept, it does not record Martha weeping over Lazarus. Was that because she didn't care? No, it was because Martha cared. She saw, I believe, her role as being strong for others. The Lord in His first meeting with her told her she was troubled and anxious about many things. I don't think that was a selfish occupation. I think she carried the troubles of others. She is a vivid illustration of the ability of godly women to be self-sacrificing and practical in times of crisis. Her instinct was to care. It is a costly and beautiful instinct.

But, like Peter, she also found it incredibly difficult not to intervene when she thought the Lord was making a mistake. Her faith in the Saviour clashed with her life experience. We often highlight Martha's failure to understand the power of the

Lord Jesus: we can excel at highlighting the faults of others. But how often do we act in precisely the same way? Our faith in the Saviour is not in question. But resting and living in that faith at critical times in our lives is the real test. When Jesus wept, the people did not doubt that He loved Lazarus. They saw how much Jesus loved His friend. But they doubted His power over death: "Could not this Man, who opened the eyes of the blind, also have kept this man from dying?" (John 11:37). Martha and Mary both believed if Jesus had been there in time, Lazarus would not have died, as though distance made Jesus less powerful. Only, Martha said, "But even now I know that whatever You ask of God, God will give You" (John 11:22).

But when the test came, she found herself saying what everyone else was thinking, "What is the Lord doing?" It is a question I have to admit I have asked many times. The Lord does not condemn Martha. The Lord is never surprised by our frailties. The Lord does not say to Martha, "I told you, Martha, I am the resurrection and the life, but you didn't listen." He says, "Did I not say to you that if you would believe you would see the glory of God?" (verse 40). He directed her faith to Himself with the promise of seeing the glory of God in the Person of Jesus as He raised her brother from the dead.

The Lord uses Martha to teach us not only to know He is the resurrection and the life but, by living faith, to know this power through all life's experiences; "that I may know Him and the power of His resurrection ..." (see Philippians 3:7-11).

Day 15

Martha serves

Then, six days before the Passover, Jesus came to Bethany, where Lazarus was who had been dead, whom He had raised from the dead. There they made Him a supper; and Martha served, but Lazarus was one of those who sat at the table with Him. Then Mary took a pound of very costly oil of spikenard, anointed the feet of Jesus, and wiped His feet with her hair. And the house was filled with the fragrance of the oil. (John 12:1-3)

The story of Martha begins and ends with a meal for Jesus. On both occasions He was the guest of honour. In the journey between those meals, we see a beautiful transformation. This morning we see peace where there had been trouble and anxiety. In place of discord, there is harmony. Martha's strenuous activity and questioning mind are no longer evident. Instead, calm and joyful sacrifice are expressed; "Martha served."

The Spirit of God records in the meal at Bethany the great features of true Christianity. Christ the centre: "There they made Him a supper." Sacrificial service: "Martha served." Fellowship: "Lazarus … sat at the table with Him." And worship: "Mary took a pound of very costly oil of spikenard, anointed the feet of Jesus, and wiped His feet with her hair. And the house was filled with the fragrance of the oil."

The place the Lord occupies in our hearts determines the value and power of our service. We must never underestimate the importance the Lord places on true service that has Him as its model. Paul reminds us in Hebrews 13:16, "But do not forget to do good and to share, for with such sacrifices, God is well pleased."

We are in a fellowship of life in Christ. Our experience of this fellowship comes from communion with Jesus, "the Resurrection and the Life". The closer we are to Him, the closer we are to each other.

Worship pours from hearts overwhelmed by Christ's love and grace. Mary, in complete silence, powerfully expressed this as she anointed the Saviour's feet, and the fragrance filled the house.

In the Old Testament the priests were never allowed to anoint themselves with incense. But every time incense was burned, its fragrance rested on them. When they left the house of God, people would be aware of it and benefit from it.

The fragrance of the oil, with which Mary in worship anointed the feet of the Lord, filled the house. In that atmosphere, it rested too on Martha, Lazarus and Mary, both inside and outside their home. May this be our experience too.

Day 16

Thursday 02 April 2020

Start writing

That which was from the beginning, which we have heard, which we have seen with our eyes, which we have looked upon, and our hands have handled, concerning the Word of life—the life was manifested, and we have seen, and bear witness, and declare to you that eternal life which was with the Father and was manifested to us—that which we have seen and heard we declare to you, that you also may have fellowship with us; and truly our fellowship is with the Father and with His Son Jesus Christ. And these things we write to you that your joy may be full. (1 John 1:1-4)

Yesterday we thought about Mary pouring a pound of precious oil of spikenard on the feet of Jesus. I have been thinking about things that I own which are precious. Here is one such thing: it's a small box full of index cards. Most are old and a bit battered. With one or two exceptions all are handwritten. (I am not noted for the quality of my handwriting!).

Last night I opened my box to get the telephone numbers of two old friends, one in Edinburgh and one in Manchester. I am always amazed when I pick up one of my cards. When I read the name, memories of their friendship and fellowship flood into my mind. How is it that a handwritten note can convey so much and immediately lift the spirit?

The Apostle John was probably the youngest of the Lord's disciples and lived to be the oldest. He uses the word "write" more than all the New Testament writers. In the opening verses of his Gospel, John writes of the glorious deity of the Lord Jesus. At the start of his first letter, which we have just read, he writes of the Saviour the apostles had seen, heard and handled, and of the fellowship they had with the Father and His Son, Jesus Christ. John embraces his fellow believers in that fellowship of life. And how did he do that? By writing to them.

There is something special about taking the time to write to family, friends and our neighbours. It costs in terms of time and thought. But it is a ministry which has value. Like prayer, it is something we can all do. To let others know they are in our thoughts, our hearts and our prayers is a precious thing. This is especially so in the present situation when we can't visit or travel. And for those who are most isolated, not able to use modern technology, or who suffer from deafness, it is so encouraging. Children love to receive letters and cards. And they reply!

I am always shocked when June presents me with the bill for buying stamps! Then I calm down, remembering the importance of writing letters and cards.

Today we can thank God for being able to communicate in so many remarkable ways. But let us never forget that God conveyed the majesty of His Person, and the depths of His grace and love in the Lord Jesus, by moving the hearts and lives of His servants over thousands of years to pick up a pen and write for Him.

Day 17

The joy of the Lord

And Jesus said to him, "Assuredly, I say to you, today you will be with Me in Paradise." (Luke 23:43)

Then I looked, and I heard the voice of many angels around the throne, the living creatures, and the elders; and the number of them was ten thousand times ten thousand, and thousands of thousands, saying with a loud voice:

"Worthy is the Lamb who was slain
To receive power and riches and wisdom,
And strength and honour and glory and blessing!"
(Revelation 5:11-12)

The story of the dying thief always moves us. The Lord Jesus, while He was dying for the whole world, found one lost sheep. He promised, not merely that he would be in Paradise, but that he would be with the Lord in Paradise.

It struck me a little while ago that I had missed something in this beautiful story of grace. I had overlooked what the Lord felt in His heart. As the Lord Jesus endured the cross and all that it meant, He heard a voice. It was not the voice of His family or His disciples. Nor was it the voices of those who expressed absolute rejection of and hatred for the Lord Jesus. It was the voice of the dying thief. Out of the recognition of where his sin had brought him, he expressed the perfection of Jesus: "This man has done nothing wrong" (Luke 23:41). Then in simple faith, he asks, "Lord, remember me when You come into Your kingdom" (Luke 23:42). The full title of Jesus above the cross was, "Jesus of Nazareth, the king of the Jews" (John 19:19). The dying thief was the single voice that acknowledged the Lord Jesus in all the power of His perfection and lowliness as Man, and the holy dignity of the One who we know is the King of kings, and Lord of lords.

What joy those words must have brought to the Lord's heart. He spoke about this joy to tax collectors and sinners in Luke 15:6: "Rejoice with me, for I have found my sheep which was lost!"

In Revelation 5:11 the Lord hears the voices of "ten thousand times ten thousand, and thousands of thousands". It's so difficult for us to grasp in our minds or hearts the wonder of that day. I think when the Lord Jesus hears the vast chorus of heaven, He will listen to each voice of personal tribute from the hearts of His redeemed people as they express holy worship and the joy that He has brought us to where He is. In the meantime, He is with us where we are. And we have the privilege each day, before the whole of creation owns Him as Lord, to worship, serve and follow Him.

Day 18

He cares for you

No one cares for my soul. (Psalm 142:4)

Casting all your care upon Him, for He cares for you. (1 Peter 5:7)

Therefore take heed to yourselves and to all the flock, among which the Holy Spirit has made you overseers, to shepherd the church of God which He purchased with His own blood. (Acts 20:28)

For all the law is fulfilled in one word, even in this: "You shall love your neighbour as yourself." (Galatians 5:14)

It costs to care. Psalm 142:4 poignantly describes what it cost the Lord Jesus. He knew what it was for no one to care for Him. It is extraordinary that while Jesus experienced this suffering, heightened by Peter words "I do not know Him", that the Lord turns to look at His dear disciple. It was a look that broke Peter's heart. In that single moment, the Lord conveyed the reality of His care for Peter that He had expressed not long before, "But I have prayed for you" (Luke 22:32).

We often read the Word of God without thinking of the profound experiences that shaped the saints that wrote it in the power of the Holy Spirit. Peter wrote, "casting all your care upon Him, for He cares for you" (1 Peter 5:7). He did not write a platitude. He wrote from the depth of his soul about the reality and power of the Saviour's care experienced at the time of Peter's greatest need.

The care Peter experienced was something he was called to express in his own ministry. The Lord asked him to feed His lambs, shepherd His sheep and feed His sheep.

Paul had the same experience. The man who wreaked havoc upon the Church of Christ became the apostle who cared so intensely for his fellow believers. In Acts 20 Paul speaks to the Ephesian elders for the last time. The first thing he says is, "Therefore take heed to yourselves" (verse 28). Our primary responsibility is to care for our own souls by placing ourselves in the care of the Lord. Today we are really concerned about our physical health and the great danger we face. We are doing everything we can to take care of ourselves. We are distancing ourselves to stay healthy. May we be daily concerned about our own spiritual health and habitually entering the presence of God and abiding in the Lord Jesus. In doing so, He equips us to care for others. We become caring by being in the presence of the Carer. He teaches us to care especially for those God has placed in our sphere of responsibility and influence, our families and fellow believers. It is from this spiritual base we are also able to care for and love our neighbours. The blessings He pours into our hearts are intended to flow out as widely as possible – "My cups runs over!"

Day 19

He came to Nazareth

So He came to Nazareth, where He had been brought up. And as His custom was, He went into the synagogue on the Sabbath day, and stood up to read. And He was handed the book of the prophet Isaiah. And when He had opened the book, He found the place where it was written: "The Spirit of the Lord is upon Me / Because He has anointed Me / To preach the gospel to the poor / He has sent Me to heal the brokenhearted / To proclaim liberty to the captives / And recovery of sight to the blind / To set at liberty those who are oppressed / To proclaim the acceptable year of the Lord." Then He closed the book, and gave it back to the attendant and sat down. And the eyes of all who were in the synagogue were fixed on Him. (Luke 4:16-20)*

I am always amazed when I read the words, "So He came to Nazareth, where He had been brought up." Nazareth, the place which Nathaniel doubted any good could come out of, was the town where the Son of God, who occupied Eternity, grew up. He was never ashamed of His title, Jesus of Nazareth. This name was the one He was known by during His ministry. It was the name written upon His cross. And, as Paul recalls in Acts 22:8, it was the name He used in resurrection glory when He spoke to Saul on the road to Damascus.

In Nazareth Jesus read from Isaiah about the beautiful aspects of His brief three-year ministry in Israel. This ministry proved who Jesus was. And its pathway of healing led to Calvary and His death as the Saviour of the world. It touched my heart some years ago to realise that the sufferings the Lord Jesus released people from during His ministry are poignant reminders of His sufferings for my salvation.

To preach the gospel to the poor – He became poor. "For you know the grace of our Lord Jesus Christ, that though He was rich, yet for your sakes He became poor, that you through His poverty might become rich" (2 Corinthians 8:9).

To heal the broken-hearted – He was broken-hearted. "Reproach has broken my heart / And I am full of heaviness / I looked for someone to take pity, but there was none / And for comforters, but I found none" (Psalm 69:20).

To set people free from disaster, the devil, disease and death – He was bound. "And when they had bound Him, they led Him away and delivered Him to Pontius Pilate, the governor" (Matthew 27:2).

To give sight to blind – He was blindfolded. "And having blindfolded Him, they struck Him on the face and asked Him, saying, 'Prophesy! Who is the one who struck You?'" (Luke 22:64).

To relieve the oppressed – He was oppressed. "He was oppressed and He was afflicted" (Isaiah 53:7).

To proclaim acceptance – He was rejected.

> "He is despised and rejected by men,
> A Man of sorrows and acquainted with grief.
> And we hid, as it were, our faces from Him;
> He was despised, and we did not esteem Him" (Isaiah 53:3).

When the Lord had finished reading from Isaiah, everyone in the synagogue was looking steadfastly at Jesus. At the beginning of this new week may our eyes be fixed on Jesus.

> "For it is the God who commanded light to shine out of darkness, who has shone in our hearts to give the light of the knowledge of the glory of God in the face of Jesus Christ" (2 Corinthians 4:6).

Day 20

Monday 06 April 2020

The power of Christ the Servant

---

*On the same day, when evening had come, He said to them,
"Let us cross over to the other side." Now when they had left the
multitude, they took Him along in the boat as He was.*

(Mark 4:35-36)

When I first became a Christian, my father told the owner of
the bakery where he worked about my new-found faith in the
Lord Jesus. A little time later, the owner came to our house
to give me an Emmaus Bible Study Course on the Gospel of
Mark. It's a great thing to show an interest and care for those
young in the faith and I have never forgotten this kindness.
The book stimulated me to study the Word of God as I learned
about Jesus being the Servant of God in the Gospel of Mark.

Mark writes in chapters 4 and 5 of the power of Christ's service
in four distinct ways. Mark describes the Lord Jesus' power over
disaster, the devil, disease, and death.

What has always impressed me is the way Mark begins this
narrative with the words "they took Jesus along in the boat as
He was" (Mark 4:36). These few words are often overlooked but
are so important. Mark describes the Lord Jesus, who had spent
Himself in ministering to multitudes, being helped into a boat
by His disciples and falling fast asleep. He paints a picture of an
exhausted Servant. It was from this place of apparent weakness
that the Lord awoke to demonstrate His astonishing power by
stilling the storm, delivering Legion, healing the desperately ill
lady and by raising Jairus' daughter from the dead.

Mark himself experienced a time in his own life when the service he undertook became too much for him, and he returned from the mission field. He must have felt a deep sense of failure. Paul was not willing to take him on another missionary journey. Instead, Barnabas took Mark to Cyprus, probably to his own home. Nearing the end of his life, Paul writes to Timothy, "Get Mark and bring him with you, for he is very useful to me for ministry" (2 Timothy 4:11, ESV).

Jesus, though all-powerful, knew the pressure and demands of service. He knew, as the Servant of God, weariness, sorrow, tears, distress, suffering and death. These were means through which He demonstrated the power and majesty of His love and grace. He understands the times when we are overwhelmed and at the end of our strength. And He moves the hearts of those who can best help us. There are times when we need a Barnabas, and there are times when we need to be a Barnabas.

May the Lord use the present crisis to make us more tender-hearted and responsive to those needs He wants us to address.

Day 21

Hannah the mother of Samuel

But Samuel ministered before the Lord, even as a child, wearing a linen ephod. Moreover his mother used to make him a little robe, and bring it to him year by year when she came up with her husband to offer the yearly sacrifice. (1 Samuel 2:18-19)

Today our Prime Minister is in intensive care. Let us pray in faith for his recovery and blessing, and for God's intervention in this time of great need.

At the end of the book of Judges we read, "In those days there was no king in Israel; everyone did what was right in his own eyes" (Judges 21:25). The next book we come to is Ruth. It is a story of bitterness ending in great blessing. Ruth's faith led to the birth of the greatest king Israel ever knew, David. God continues this theme in 1 Samuel 1 with the story of Hannah. Her prayer of faith resulted in the birth of Samuel, leading to the spiritual revival of Israel and the anointing of David as the king of Israel. God used the painful experiences of Ruth and Hannah to bring about enormous blessing.

I have often reflected on how Hannah's childlessness brought her into the presence of God. There she silently prayed in her heart for a male child and God answered her prayer. But today I want to reflect on Hannah's faith as a mother. She had a mother's heart before Samuel was born and she became the mother of six children. It was such a sacrifice when Hannah fulfilled her vow to God and gave tiny Samuel to the Lord for the whole of his life. Outwardly, he was being left in the care of Eli, the head of one of the most corrupt family of priests Israel knew. But that was not where Hannah was going to leave him.

She was placing him in the care and protection of the Lord. She recalls, "For this child I prayed, and the Lord has granted me my petition which I asked of Him. Therefore I also have lent him to the Lord; as long as he lives he shall be lent to the Lord" (1 Samuel 1:27-28). Her next words are, "My heart rejoices in the Lord ..." (1 Samuel 2:1).

Why does the Spirit of God tell us "His mother used to make him a little robe, and bring it to him year by year when she came up with her husband to offer the yearly sacrifice" (1 Samuel 2:19)? Because He wanted us to know how deeply Hannah cared for her son. Her other five children did not replace Samuel. He was in her heart and service and probably in her prayers for the rest of her life.

When Samuel judged Israel he had a circuit of service covering Bethel, Gilgal and Mizpah. But then we read, "But he always returned to Ramah, for his home was there. There he judged Israel, and there he built an altar to the Lord" (1 Samuel 7:17). Ramah was where Samuel was born. It was his mother's home. Our homes are so precious.

Samuel, as an old man, anointed David king of Israel. That day he learnt a lesson his mother knew the truth of before he was born, "The Lord does not see as man sees; for man looks at the outward appearance, but the Lord looks at the heart" (1 Samuel 16:7).

In these difficult times, let us pray for Christian mothers and the unique spiritual influence of their love, faith, hope and the godly heritage they provide, expressed in their care, prayers, sacrifices, and the homes they build.

Day 22

Wednesday 08 April 2020

There is a friend …

Then He (Jesus) said to them, "My soul is exceedingly sorrowful, even to death. Stay here and watch with Me."   (Matthew 26:38)

Only Luke is with me.   (2 Timothy 4:11)

But the Lord stood with me and strengthened me.   (2 Timothy 4:17)

After the funeral of his wife, George Muller asked a friend to stay with him. He recorded that they sat together right through the night and never spoke a word. There are times in our lives when we just need the presence of friends.

The Lord Jesus had this experience. As the agony of Gethsemane and the cross lay before Him, Jesus asked Peter, James and John to stay with him and watch.

When Paul writes in 2 Timothy 4:11, "only Luke is with me", he was experiencing the loneliness and rejection of serving God as expressed in verse 16, "At my first defence no one stood with me, but all forsook me." It is touching that the one friend who was with Paul was Luke, the beloved physician. We have heard recently of doctors and nurses caring for those who are so desperately ill and without access to family. A vital part of that care is being close to those who feel so alone. Luke was a doctor when there were few drugs or treatments. On so many occasions, he must have felt helpless. But what Luke always brought was the heart of a friend.

A week last Sunday, at our first organised Zoom meeting, it was lovely to see the faces of so many friends. Among them I saw two who have been my friends for over 55 years. We have never lost fellowship in all that time. The present circumstances make us realise the value of the fellowship we enjoy and can so often take for granted. The One who brought us into this fellowship of life is the Lord Jesus, the friend who loves at all times (Proverbs 17:17).

Paul had witnessed the death of Stephen and raged against the Gospel he preached. But he heard the Church's first martyr declare, "Look! I see the heavens opened and the Son of Man standing at the right hand of God!" (Acts 7:56). The Lord Jesus stood by Stephen in all the rejection and loneliness of his painful death. He didn't take him out of the circumstances but came into his circumstances.

Towards the end of his life Paul had the same experience of the Lord Jesus: "The Lord stood with me and strengthened me, so that the message might be preached fully through me." The Lord Jesus is the friend who sticks closer than a brother (Proverbs 18:24). In doing so He strengthens us to share His love and demonstrate true friendship.

Day 23

Thursday 09 April 2020

Learning to pray

"Lord, teach us to pray".　　　　　　　　　　　　　*(Luke 11:1)*

After the Lord Jesus had finished praying one day, an unnamed disciple said to Him, "Lord, teach us to pray". I am pretty sure that all the Lord's disciples were taught, from childhood, to pray. The request, a prayer in itself, spontaneously emerged from the heart of the disciple as he watched the Saviour pray. It came from observing the Lord Jesus. It wasn't a selfish request. The disciple didn't go to the Lord privately and say, "Lord, teach me to pray". He asked for all the disciples, "Teach us to pray".

Interestingly, the Lord didn't say to the disciples, "Today, I am going to teach you to pray". No, He waited for the exercise of one heart. The disciple, moved by seeing the Lord in prayer, wanted, with all his fellow disciples, to be taught how to come to the Throne of Grace.

It is so important to allow God to speak to our hearts so that we can talk, in prayer, with Him. It is through the Word of God that we see Jesus and learn of Him. By allowing Him to minister to our hearts first, He prepares us to minister in prayer. We learn about the power of intercession by looking to the One Who ever lives to make intercession for us (Hebrews 7:25). He teaches us in prayer to lift our eyes to our Father in heaven in worship; to seek the will of God; to ask for His provision; to confess our failure; to seek the blessing of others; to know His direction and protection.

It was the Lord's custom to pray daily. There are people and things which need our constant prayers. We should never stop praying, for example, for daily direction, our children (whether young or older), family, assemblies, the Gospel and our government. We also need to pray regarding the present crisis and those suffering in it, until it is past.

In recent years we have started to pray geographically. Our prayers begin in one place and move to the next place around the UK and overseas. As we 'visit' each place in our prayers, the Lord reminds us of those for whom we should pray and also impresses on us fresh reasons for thanksgiving and intercession. Prayer is a ministry. It takes time and effort. Martin Luther once wrote, "I am so busy today; I will need to pray for at least two hours." The need for prayer increases with pressures we face. It was the custom of the Lord Jesus to go to the Garden of Gethsemane to pray. Gethsemane means, "olive press" – a place of pressure. It was there the Lord Jesus is spoken of as praying "more earnestly".

I was talking with friends recently about the way we now patiently wait in line to do shopping. Also, the other evening after clapping the NHS, we stopped to talk with neighbours and because of social distancing we had to shout to each other! This morning we won't have to queue at the Throne of Grace nor will we have to shout so that our Father can hear us. Because of what the Lord Jesus has done, we can come peacefully into His presence to pray and,

> "in everything by prayer and supplication, with thanksgiving let our requests be made known to God. And the peace of God, which surpasses all understanding, will guard your hearts and minds through Christ Jesus" (Philippians 4:6-7).

Day 24

Good Friday 10 April 2020

Thankfulness for the Saviour

"The Son of God, who loved me and gave Himself for me."

(Galatians 2:20)

Last evening the nation, once again, paused to express its thankfulness to doctors, nurses, and health professionals in the NHS in the current crisis. It is good to say thank you.

Today is Good Friday, which commemorates the death of Jesus upon the cross. We sometimes sing:

> "Thy cross, Thy cross! 'tis there we see
> What Thou, our blessed Saviour, art;
> There all the love that dwells in Thee
> Was labouring in Thy breaking heart."

I want to pause this morning and reflect upon words Jesus spoke as He died at Calvary, and bow in thankfulness to the Son of God "who loved me and gave Himself for me" (Galatians 2:20).

"Father, forgive them, for they do not know what they do" (Luke 23:34). Christ's forgiveness removes the guilt that haunts us and gives us peace with God. It is the most extraordinary experience. We can be thankful that the Lord Jesus died, so that we might be forgiven.

"Assuredly, I say to you, today you will be with Me in Paradise" (Luke 23:43). We can be thankful that no matter how far away from God we were, His love removed the distance and brought us into a place of nearness now and for eternity.

He said to His mother, "Woman, behold your son!" Then He said to the disciple, "Behold your mother!" (John 19:26-27).

On the cross the Lord Jesus demonstrated His love for the world, for the dying thief and for his mother. We can be thankful that the Lord Jesus never ceases to care for His own, and, as with John, He puts the care for others in our hearts.

"My God, My God, why have You forsaken Me?" (Matthew 27:46). The Lord's central cry from the cross described the depth of His suffering. We can be so thankful that the Lord Jesus was forsaken so we will never be forsaken.

"I thirst" (John 19:28). These words express the utter exhaustion of the Saviour in the complete giving of Himself. We can be thankful that we "know the grace of our Lord Jesus Christ, that though He was rich, yet for your sakes He became poor, that you through His poverty might become rich" (2 Corinthians 8:9).

"It is finished" (John 19:30). "Finished" is a victory cry reminding us that the work of salvation is a complete and eternal work. We can rest with thankful hearts in Christ's love, displayed at Calvary, that will never let us go.

"Father, into Your hands I commit My spirit" (Luke 23:46). The Father's name embraces all that Jesus said from the cross. He commits Himself to the Father and in resurrection spoke of ascending to "My Father and your Father" (John 20:17). We can give thanks that the Lord Jesus has brought us to His Father and that He tells us, "the Father Himself loves you" (John 16:27).

May we express our thankfulness to the Saviour by our willingness to forgive, to love our neighbours, to love our families, to sacrifice, to spend and be spent, to be victorious through faith, and to worship the Father and the Son in the power and liberty of the Holy Spirit.

Day 25

Saturday 11 April 2020

The Throne of Grace

Let us therefore come boldly to the throne of grace, that we may obtain mercy and find grace to help in time of need. (Hebrews 4:16)

When she heard about Jesus, she came behind Him in the crowd and touched His garment. For she said, "If only I may touch His clothes, I shall be made well." (Mark 5:27-28)

A brother once told me of a visit he made to Chester Zoo. He said he remembered standing in front of the lion enclosure looking at a male lion sitting majestically in the sun. Even behind the large fence that separated him from this magnificent animal, he had a sense of unease. As he watched, two lion cubs walked up to the male lion with complete confidence and sat beside him. The brother said there was a significant difference between himself and the cubs. They were the children of the powerful lion.

Boldness is not brashness. We should never come casually or carelessly into the presence of God. As the children of God, we should be characterised by dignity, confidence and a deep sense of God's glory and grace. He welcomes us through the Person and work of Christ Jesus: "But now in Christ Jesus you who once were far off have been brought near by the blood of Christ" (Ephesians 2:13). He is always ready to respond to our needs.

The story of the diseased woman in Mark chapter 5 is a beautiful illustration of salvation. She was afraid, but she still came to the Lord in simple faith. The story also illustrates the experience of God's dear children, because sometimes we come to the Lord Jesus when we are afraid and overwhelmed by our circumstances. We have no strength or confidence; we just feel our utter need and helplessness. And in those painful situations, we reach out to Him, in the weakness of our faith, to seek His presence and healing.

The Lord Jesus said to the woman, "Daughter, your faith has made you well. Go in peace, and be healed of your affliction" (Mark 5:34). The people and the disciples had no understanding of the deep need of the woman. She was just a face in the crowd. We can sometimes, in the busyness of life and even in Christian service, be unaware of the needs of our fellow believers and our neighbours. But the Lord Jesus always feels compassion towards us and responds to us individually, however small our faith may be.

Our present circumstances give us time to reflect upon the grace and power of the Saviour and the time to come before the Throne of Grace. Let us reach out to the Lord Jesus in faith. May He deepen that faith and give us to know His peace and healing, and, in doing so, make us sensitive to the needs around us to serve Him better in a broken world.

Day 26

Sunday 12 April 2020

Remember Me

We will be glad and rejoice in you. We will remember your love.
(Song of Solomon 1:4)

This is My body which is given for you: this do in remembrance of Me. Likewise also the cup after supper, saying, This cup is the new testament in My blood, which is shed for you. *(Luke 22:19-20, AV)*

For as often as you eat this bread and drink this cup, you proclaim the Lord's death till He comes. *(1 Corinthians 11:26)*

The Song of Solomon helps us to express the joy and gladness we have in the Lord Jesus by putting into words what is in our hearts this morning, "We will remember your love."

Each Sunday morning it never ceases to amaze me that, from the majesty of heaven, the Lord Jesus looks into this world with a desire in His heart to gather us together to remember Him. We think of this when we read, in this same lovely book, "Let me see your face, Let me hear your voice" (Song of Solomon 2:14).

This desire of the Lord Jesus is the same when we met in our thousands, or we met in our twos and threes. And, it is especially true this morning as, throughout the world, we meet in isolation. This isolation does not prevent the Lord of Glory embracing us as one within the reality of His eternal love and delighting in our expressions of worship. The Lord treasures our remembrance of Him. He treasures it in each of our redeemed hearts, and when those hearts join as one in the harmony of worship. The Lord Jesus established His supper on earth just before He went to the cross. He gave us the simplest of emblems to show forth His profound sacrifice of love. It is the time when we put everything else to the side and focus our minds and hearts on the glory of the journey He made to save us. It is the time when we retrace His steps to Calvary and are overwhelmed, once more, by the beauty and power of His death upon the cross. And it is the time when we speak to the Father of all the glories of His eternal Son.

As Paul writes of the Lord Jesus, in the majesty of His resurrection in heaven, re-affirming His constant desire to be remembered by His own, he adds, "For as often as you eat this bread and drink this cup, you proclaim the Lord's death till He comes" (1 Corinthians 11:26). This morning the Lord Jesus would fill our hearts with His love as we remember Him. He would fill our hearts with faith as we look up to Him where He is in glory and discover we are ever in His heart. And He would fill our hearts with hope that, one glorious day, He will return and He will take us to be with Him eternally in the Father's home.

Let us come with hearts full and ready to give voice to our thankfulness and to praise our wondrous Saviour.

Day 27

Monday 13 April 2020

Looking unto Jesus

Looking unto Jesus, the author and finisher of our faith.

(Hebrews 12:2)

I remember the first bike my father bought me. It was a little too big, so he had to put blocks on the pedals so I could reach them. I was so excited as he taught me to ride. I tried to keep my balance but didn't have much success. I was in constant danger of falling off, but all the time my father held the saddle. I remember him coming to the front of the bike and holding the handlebars, so I stayed upright. He said to me, "Gordon, you will never ride a bike until you learn to look up!" His advice had an immediate effect, and off I went feeling as if I owned a Rolls Royce.

It is the same in our Christian lives. Our spiritual power and progress are dependent upon looking up to Jesus. Too often we try to find answers within our ourselves and go our own way. That's when we lose balance, and our lives become wayward and unstable. The Lord is always there to hold the saddle, and to stop us and say, "Gordon, look up!"

"Behold the Lamb of God" were words John the Baptist said on two occasions. First he used them to declare the Lord Jesus as the "Lamb of God who takes away the sin of the world!" (John 1:29). We come to Christ by looking to Him in simple faith as our Saviour. On the second occasion, John said, "Behold the Lamb of God!" (John 1:36), and Andrew and his fellow disciple followed Jesus, had fellowship with Jesus and witnessed for Jesus. We look to Jesus for our sanctification. He wants us to abide in Him, follow Him and serve Him.

"Looking unto Jesus" are words we read in Hebrews 12:2 to encourage us to always look up in faith to Jesus. He is the source and completer of our faith. The Lord Jesus suffered in love for us. He now sits in glory and sustains us in our daily pathway of faith through the power of His endless life.

"Looking for the blessed hope and glorious appearing of our great God and Saviour Jesus Christ, who gave Himself for us, that He might redeem us from every lawless deed and purify for Himself His own special people, zealous for good works" (Titus 2:13-14). With these words the Spirit of God encourages us to be looking for the return of the Lord Jesus for His people, as is described in 1 Thessalonians 4. And – to be looking for "His glorious appearing" as the King of kings and Lord of lords when every knee shall bow to Him and every tongue "confess that Jesus Christ is Lord, to the glory of God the Father" (Philippians 2:11). John explains that "everyone who has this hope in Him (Jesus) purifies himself, just as He is pure" (1 John 3:3). The reality of this hope transforms our lives.

"We, according to His promise, look for new heavens and a new earth in which righteousness dwells" (2 Peter 3:13). Through Peter's words, God causes us to look beyond Christ's millennial reign, during which righteousness reigns, to the eternal state and the Day of God when He fulfils all His purposes of love and grace in Christ, and righteousness abides.

God took Moses to Mount Nebo and the top of Pisgah to view all the land of Israel. The Father takes us by the hand and by His Spirit to the Lord Jesus to view eternity.

Day 28

Tuesday 14 April 2020

The Jericho Walk

But a certain Samaritan, as he journeyed, came where he was.
And when he saw him, he had compassion.   *(Luke 10:33)*

And when Jesus came to the place, He looked up and saw him,
and said to him, "Zacchaeus, make haste and come down, for
today I must stay at your house." So he made haste and came
down, and received Him joyfully.   *(Luke 19:5-6)*

Most days, like so many others, I go out for a walk. I call it my "Jericho walk" because nearly everyone I meet crosses over to the other side of the road. I've started doing it myself! Of course, unlike the priest and Levite in Luke 10, we don't cross the road because we don't care about each other. No, we do it because we do care about each other's health and well-being.

The road from Jerusalem to Jericho, the lowest city on earth, is about 18 miles long, descending from about 2500 feet (760 metres) above to around 800 feet (250 metres) below sea level. But Jericho is not about distance; it's about nearness.

The story of the Good Samaritan is a great encouragement for us to show compassion to people in desperate need. But I believe the Lord Jesus wasn't speaking primarily about our behaviour. He was talking about the journey He took to save us. God chose priests and Levites to minister the compassion and love of God and to bring people near to Him. Instead, self-righteousness and selfishness caused them to distance themselves from their neighbours at times of greatest need. The man on the road to Jericho lost everything he had. It was the Samaritan, a striking picture of the Lord Jesus as the rejected stranger in this world,

67

who came to where the man was to save him. The Lord Jesus didn't come in the royal robes of a king or dressed as a priest. He came clothed in lowliness and grace to redeem us, and to pour His joy and the Holy Spirit into our hearts. Then to place us in a fellowship of life where we experience His continued care. In doing so, He asks us to be like Him and display His compassionate love.

In Luke 19 Jesus is not telling a parable. He was actually in Jericho, surrounded, as He often was, by a crowd of people. He stopped beneath a sycamore tree. And there, in the lowest city on Earth, the Son of God, who came from the highest place in heaven, looked up into the tree to see Zacchaeus. That moment captures the wonder of the grace of God – the Son of God in the lowest place looking up to a man in the greatest need. Zacchaeus was not beaten and left half-dead. He still had all his possessions. He was not abandoned. But in his heart, despite all he owned, he was lost, and Jesus came to save him. Jesus looked up and said, "Zacchaeus, make haste and come down, for today I must stay at your house" (Luke 19:5). Zacchaeus did not need asking twice. He rushed to come down and joyfully receive the Lord.

Sometimes the Lord's ministry is to lift us up, and sometimes it is to bring us down, but it is always so that we might know Him and become like Him.

Day 29

Wednesday 15 April 2020

Always rejoicing

Rejoice in the Lord always. Again I will say, rejoice! (Philippians 4:4)

Isolation is tough. Some days are better than others, but we struggle with being confined. We are not used to being without friends and family and the freedom to interact in the world we live in. God did not make us to be alone or isolated.

I don't think there is a book in the New Testament which is so full of joy as Paul's letter to the Philippians. Every chapter of this precious book speaks of rejoicing in the Lord in some way. But it was written from prison. Some twenty years before, Paul and Silas had sat beaten, bleeding and bound in the stocks of the innermost cell of the jail in Philippi. And, at the darkest hour of the night, their voices had soared up in prayer and praises to God.

That experience of prayer and praise still filled the heart of the apostle as he wrote to his dear friends, ones who cared for him more than any other of the saints amongst whom Paul had ministered the grace of God. But how could he maintain such a joyous spirit and love for others? He tells us how in each chapter of his letter:

"For to me, to live is Christ" (Philippians 1:21).

Paul had the life of Christ. He had learned day by day that both freedom and imprisonment were circumstances God used to express his life in Christ. He writes in chapter 1 that his chains in Christ were a witness to the whole palace guard. Paul's imprisonment became the means of demonstrating that the Son of God had made him free. He wasn't simply alive; he was fully experiencing "life more abundant".

"Let this mind be in you which was also in Christ Jesus" (Philippians 2:5).

Paul had the mind of Christ. He responded daily to the Lord Jesus' invitation: "Come to Me, all you who labour and are heavy laden, and I will give you rest. Take My yoke upon you and learn from Me, for I am gentle and lowly in heart, and you will find rest for your souls. For My yoke is easy and My burden is light" (Matthew 11:28-30).

"That I may know Him" (Philippians 3:10).

Paul had the knowledge of Christ. For the apostle, the experiences of each day were fresh opportunities to deepen his knowledge of Christ. It wasn't intellectual knowledge; it was imparted by the operation of the Holy Spirit in his heart to keep him abiding and growing in Christ.

"I can do all things through Christ who strengthens me" (Philippians 4:13).

Paul drew on the strength of Christ. There was a time when we were without strength (Romans 5:6). But in love Christ died and rose again for us. Now, like Paul, we can draw, every day and in every circumstance, from the strength of our risen Saviour and Lord, and respond to Him in worship and service.

> "And my God shall supply all your need according to His riches in glory by Christ Jesus. Now to our God and Father be glory for ever and ever. Amen" (Philippians 4:19-20).

Day 30

My Father's business

"Did you not know that I must be about My Father's business?"

(Luke 2:49)

Only Luke tells us about Jesus when, as a twelve-year-old boy, Mary and Joseph found Him in the temple at Jerusalem. The story tells us how much they cared for their young son as they desperately searched for Him. It conveys the relief they experienced when they found Jesus. Of course, He was not lost! He was, as He explained, doing His Father's business in His Father's house.

Luke also records in this chapter the wonder of the incarnation when the angel announced the birth, in the city of David, of the Saviour, Christ the Lord (verse 11). He goes on to tell us Simeon's words, "My eyes have seen Your salvation" (verse 30) and of the witness of Anna. Afterwards, Mary and Joseph settled in Nazareth, and their lives became ordinary. No more angels, or extraordinary dreams, or surprising visits by shepherds and wise men. They lived the everyday lives of a working-class family in a quiet home in a poor town. We are told in verse 19 that, after the birth of Jesus, Mary kept the memory of all these things in her heart and reflected on them. But in verse 50 we read they did not understand what Jesus said. But again His mother treasured up all these things in her heart.

Had Mary and Joseph forgotten Who was living with them? If they had, Mary's heart was re-ignited. I have to ask myself, "Do I forget Who lives with me day by day?" Does my heart need re-igniting?

The Lord was surprised they did not know He must be doing His Father's business. But what was that business? Luke describes it for us. Jesus was sitting amongst the teachers, listening to them, asking them questions, understanding and providing remarkable answers.

Only Luke records, in the last chapter of his gospel, the resurrected Saviour on the road to Emmaus. Jesus was still doing His Father's business. He was still with those He cared for, He was still listening to their questions, He was still asking them questions, and He was still conveying His understanding and remarkable answers. I believe the Lord Jesus continues this ministry in glory. We were not there in the temple or able to walk with Him to Emmaus. But He lives, through His blessed Holy Spirit, in our hearts, and we can know the joy of His presence and power both in the ordinariness and extraordinariness of life's journey.

After the disciples' experience of the Lord Jesus' presence in Luke 24, we read in verses 32-33: "And they said to one another, 'Did not our heart burn within us while He talked with us on the road, and while He opened the Scriptures to us?' So they rose up that very hour and returned to Jerusalem." It is the realisation of the presence of the Lord Jesus and His words of love and grace which re-ignite our hearts in love for Him. He also energises us to serve Him and take action to convey His love and grace to others.

Day 31

Friday 17 April 2020

Jacob at Bethel: The grace of God

"Behold, I am with you and will keep you wherever you go, and will bring you back to this land; for I will not leave you until I have done what I have spoken to you." *(Genesis 28:15)*

It is difficult to find a more vivid picture of the grace of God in the Old Testament than we do in the story of Jacob. As this man's life unfolds, there is little to attract us to him. He was called Jacob because he held onto the heel of Esau, his twin brother, as they were born. His name means "supplanter". And although he was a quiet man, he ruthlessly took advantage of Esau to obtain his birthright and conspired with his mother to rob Esau of his father's blessing for his firstborn. As a consequence, he fled for his life.

For the first time in his life, alone, and with an uncertain future ahead of him, Jacob falls asleep with a rock for a pillow. It is at this moment God appears to him in a dream. There are many things we would have expected God to address in Jacob's life. The God of righteousness would have to deal with Jacob's character and behaviour and where it had led him. God would indeed deal with those features of his life. But He does not begin there. God begins, not with who Jacob was, but Who He is; the God of all grace.

All Jacob's life was consumed by chasing things which did not belong to him. When God speaks to Jacob, He says, "I am the Lord God … I will give you … I am with you … I will keep you … I will bring you back … I will not leave you … I have spoken" (verses 13, 15). God poured out the richness of His grace on Jacob with holy tenderness and promise. When Jacob awoke from his dream, he took the stone he had rested on and set it up as a pillar and poured oil on top of it. Then he made a vow which began with the words, "If God …". Everything he mentioned next was about material things. Then finally, he promises to give back to God a tenth of what God would give him.

In Luke 15 when the Prodigal Son returned in repentance to his father's house, he discovered what he had never understood before – just how much his father loved him. His brother never left his father's house and never understood his father's love. Jacob had yet to learn how much God loved him.

I have to ask myself why it is that I often fail to understand the greatness of the love and grace of God. He never asked Jacob for sacrifice, vows or money. He did not ask Jacob for anything. He does not deal with me based on who I am. He deals with me on the ground of His eternal love displayed through free grace. He doesn't ask me to pay him back, as if I could, or make impossible vows. He asks me to trust Him and live each day of my life in the majesty of His transforming grace in the Person of the Lord Jesus Christ.

Jacob had a long way to travel and many lessons to learn: so do we. His life seemed like a rollercoaster and, at times, so can ours. But there is one glorious constant, one never-changing assurance for us to rest in:

> "Behold, I am with you and will keep you wherever you go, and will bring you back to this land; for I will not leave you until I have done what I have spoken to you" (Genesis 28:15).

Day 32

Jacob at Penuel: The blessing of God

"I will not let You go unless You bless me!"   (Genesis 32:26)

Jacob was in the house of Laban, his uncle, for twenty years. He spent those years under the authority of a man who was shrewder and more materialistic than Jacob ever was. God taught him some bitter lessons during that time; he also learned about the faithfulness of God's promise, "I am with you" (Genesis 28:15). God also fulfilled His promise to take Jacob safely home.

He returned home as the wealthy head of a large family. At the brook Jabbok he sent his wives, children, household and great possessions ahead of him. And he stood alone once more. He must have remembered the day when he was alone at Bethel, and God spoke to him of His marvellous grace.

This time God did not speak to him in a dream from heaven. Instead, He came down to Jacob and wrestled with him (Genesis 32:24-31). This unusual event conveys all the struggles that were in Jacob's life and was the means God used to bring him into blessing. The woman in Mark 5 discovered the power of the Lord Jesus in a simple touch. God did not throw Jacob to the ground to end Jacob's struggles. No, He touched Jacob's hip, and he was helpless. Then, just as like Jesus on the road to Emmaus, God "made as though He would have gone further". But Jacob cries, "I will not let You go unless You bless me!" (Genesis 32:26). This cry expressed the need that had always been in Jacob's heart. He had sought blessing by being ruthless and cheating his brother. He had experienced the goodness of God as he struggled in Laban's house. But there was something more he needed. God's question is powerful. "What is your name?" (Genesis 32:27). God knew Jacob's name. He wanted Jacob to know it. Why? Because it conveyed everything he was naturally. It summed him up as a man. He answers, "Jacob". And God immediately responded by giving him the new name "Israel". In response, Jacob asks God His name. But God says, "Why is it that you ask about My name?" (Genesis 32:29). And God blesses him. God was, as it were, saying to Jacob, "You know Me. You met Me at Bethel. I was with you all those difficult years in Laban's house, and I am with you now." The difference was that Jacob saw God face to face. He understood at last that we find true blessing in the presence of God. He loves and cares for us and wants us to know the reality of His presence every day of our lives. Job wrote at the end of his struggles with suffering and pain:

> "I have heard of You by the hearing of the ear,
> But now my eye sees You" (Job 42:5).

Jacob called the place Peniel because he had seen God face to face. From that day onward, every step Jacob took was a reminder that God had blessed him. He knew his weakness, and he knew the power of God in that weakness. Many more struggles and much suffering awaited Jacob. But he was transformed by the blessing of God's presence into a person who blessed others. Jacob blessed Pharaoh and he blessed his own children and grandchildren. In Hebrews 11:21 Jacob, the man who began his life so far from God, ended his life so close to God. He worshipped leaning on his shepherd's staff and blessed his children in the name of God, who had shepherded him all the days of his life. "The Lord is my Shepherd" (Psalm 23:1).

Day 33

Sunday 19 April 2020

The Powerful Shepherd

"Therefore My Father loves Me, because I lay down My life that I may take it again. No one takes it from Me, but I lay it down of Myself. I have power to lay it down, and I have power to take it again. This command I have received from My Father."

(John 10:17-18)

The Old Testament has some remarkable illustrations of Jesus the Saviour. Adam's deep sleep reminds us of Christ loving the Church and how He gave Himself for her. Isaac on Mount Moriah reminds us of Christ's complete obedience and devotion to the Father's will. Joseph reminds us of the rejection of Jesus by His brethren, and His subsequent suffering and glory. And the Passover lamb reminds us of Jesus as the Lamb of God and the perfection of His sacrifice. All these beautiful pictures are passive in character. It was God who caused Adam's sleep; Abraham, who took Isaac; Joseph's brothers sold Joseph; the families in Egypt sacrificed the Passover lamb. But there is one person who presents the Lord Jesus in all the power of the Good Shepherd coming to save His sheep: David.

In 1 Samuel 16, when Samuel came to Bethlehem to anoint a new king to replace Saul, David wasn't even present. Why? Because he was keeping his father's sheep. Psalm 78:70-72 recalls how God called him from the sheepfolds. In 1 Samuel 17, before we get to the end of the story of David and Goliath, we are told David fed his father's sheep in Bethlehem (verse 15). In verse 20 we learn that he left those sheep with a keeper. Eliab, David's oldest brother, tries to belittle David (verse 28) by asking with whom David had left the few sheep in the wilderness. When

Saul points out to David that he had never been a soldier, David recalls how he had saved his sheep from the lion and the bear. These verses present David as one who had the heart of a loving and fearless shepherd, a shepherd who was prepared to lay down his life for his father's sheep. David is an illustration of the Good Shepherd.

When David went down into the Valley of Elah, there was no hesitation or caution in meeting Goliath. It is a picture of power. He ran quickly toward the giant and killed him with a single stone and without a sword in his hand. David is a vivid Old Testament illustration of the power of the Lord Jesus as the Good Shepherd who said, "Therefore My Father loves Me, because I lay down My life that I may take it again. No one takes it from Me, but I lay it down of Myself. I have power to lay it down, and I have power to take it again. This command I have received from My Father" (John 10:17-18).

Now there is one flock and one all-powerful Shepherd – the powerful Good Shepherd Who loved us and died for us, the powerful Great Shepherd Who rose again and lives for us in heaven now, and the powerful Chief Shepherd Who will come for us and ultimately reign as King of kings and Lord of lords.

Before David came to the throne of Israel, his followers owned him as their lord and their king. The Spirit came on Amasai to declare,

> "We are yours, O David; We are on your side …"
> (1 Chronicles 12:18)

Now we have a fresh opportunity each day to worship, follow and serve our all-powerful Saviour:

> "Lord we are Thine: Thy claims we own,
> Ourselves to Thee we'd wholly give."
> (J. G. Deck)

Day 34

Monday 20 April 2020

Barley loaves and small fish

"There is a lad here who has five barley loaves and two small fish, but what are they among so many?" (John 6:9)

The feeding of the five thousand teaches us some simple but essential lessons about discipleship and faith. Towards the end of chapter 1 of the Gospel of John we read about the Lord calling Philip to follow Him. Later, in John's account of the feeding of the five thousand, we see the Lord developing Philip's discipleship. He does this with a testing problem, where could they buy enough to feed so many people. Notice that the Lord uses the word "we". He includes Himself in the problem. Philip gave his honest assessment which, summed up, meant, "Lord, we can't do it." Then Andrew got involved and introduced someone: "There is a lad here who has five barley loaves and two small fish, but what are they among so many?" The bread was just barley loaves, the common food of the poor, and the fish were small. Andrew was saying, "We have something, but the problem is overwhelming." Philip and Andrew looked at the largeness of the problem and the smallness of the resources. They looked in the wrong direction. I know I have often had the same experience. But then there was the lad who brought the five barley loaves and the two small fish.

When my eldest granddaughter was very young, I took her with me to buy some wood. When we got back home, I got ready to unload the heavy timber. She said to me, "I'll help you, grandad", and she got hold of one end of a large piece of wood. There was no way she could carry the load, but as I took the weight, she held tightly at the other end! Children, as the Lord

Jesus points out, teach us so much about faith. The Lord does not expect us to solve problems: He wants us to bring them to Him. Philip and Andrew had witnessed the Lord turn water into wine, and it says the disciples believed in Him (John 2:11). But in chapter 6, as they saw the crowds, their faith deserted them and they said, "Lord, this can't be done." I doubt the boy had ever seen a miracle, but he came to Jesus with his childlike faith, tiny resources and a heart that said, "Lord, you can do this."

The Lord still tests us. He comes close to us and asks, "What shall we do?" He looks for that joyous and victorious faith that looks to Him and places our weakness in His hands to demonstrate His power and blessing.

The Lord took the barley loaves and gave thanks to the Father for them. Our faith always rejoices the Lord's heart.

Day 35

Tuesday 21 April 2020

Being in a basket

Then the disciples took him by night and let him down through the wall in a large basket. *(Acts 9:25)*

Paul wrote to the Philippians about his background: "Circumcised the eighth day, of the stock of Israel, of the tribe of Benjamin, a Hebrew of the Hebrews; concerning the law, a Pharisee; concerning zeal, persecuting the church; concerning the righteousness which is in the law, blameless."

(Philippians 3:5-6 also see Acts 22:3)

If his Jewish friends of years gone by could have seen Saul (as he was called then) being let down the walls of Damascus in a basket, what would they have thought? They may have wondered: "How did this gifted, privileged, influential, zealous young man with such a bright future before him, come to this?" But how different the truth was.

Saul became the apostle Paul and would go on to discover what it was like to be in prison. But being in a basket against the wall of a great city was a unique experience in his life. In that tiny space, he gradually descended the high walls of Damascus. As he did so, he was in danger of being discovered, of the rope snapping and of his helpers not being able to bear his weight.

When Saul arrived in Damascus, after the Lord Jesus had met him from heaven on the road to the city, he was blind. The Lord Jesus sent Ananias to heal him of his blindness. The first recorded words he heard before seeing anyone were, "Brother Saul." And he found himself in a fellowship of love with the very people he had come to Damascus to destroy. Then because of his immediate and bold witness to the Lord Jesus, he became the hunted instead of the hunter. It was amongst the unnamed disciples of the Lord Jesus at Damascus that Saul learned the love of Christ. And it was those same disciples who placed him in a basket and let him down the walls of the city to save his life.

We do not know what Saul was thinking in the course of that short but dangerous journey. But there are things that journey teaches us. We learn that God sometimes confines us to protect us. We learn that we are in a fellowship of life. We begin to understand that, however gifted, resourceful and knowledgeable we think we may be, we shall always need the prayers and the support of our fellow brothers and sisters in Christ. Ananias explained that the Lord Jesus chose Paul to serve Him in the most remarkable way. But that night, in that basket, he was entirely dependent on the kindness and love of those he once hated.

Paul never forgot the way he had persecuted the Church of Christ, calling himself the "chief of sinners" (1 Timothy 1:15). But once he became a brother in Christ, he never stopped valuing, protecting and building up the Body of Christ. On the way to Damascus, the Lord Jesus Christ displayed His love from glory. In Damascus, the Lord Jesus revealed His love in the lives of His people. Today He still wants to do that.

Day 36

Wednesday 22 April 2020

Sleeping beneath the wings of God

That night Peter was sleeping, bound with two chains between two soldiers; and the guards before the door were keeping the prison.
(Acts 12:6)

There was once a competition inviting artists to paint a scene that expressed peace. There were lots of beautiful paintings of sunsets, landscapes and calm water. But the painting which won the competition was very surprising. It was a painting of a tree lashed with rain on a dark, stormy night. It was difficult to see what the painting had to do with peace until you looked closer. There, in one of the branches, was a bird's nest with fledglings nestled fast asleep beneath their mother's wings.

The New Testament records Peter sleeping on three occasions. The first time, alongside his two friends James and John, he fell asleep on the Mount of Transfiguration. The Lord had taken them up the mountain to see His glory, and they fell asleep. On the second occasion, the Lord Jesus took the three friends with Him into the Garden of Gethsemane. He wanted them to be with Him in His hour of greatest need, and they fell asleep. I have to ask myself how often I am asleep to the sufferings and glory of the Lord Jesus.

But in the two letters he wrote by the Spirit of God towards the end of his life, Peter speaks of the sufferings of Christ and the glories that would follow (1 Peter 1:11). He remembers, as if it was yesterday, that he and his friends "were eyewitnesses of His majesty" (2 Peter 1:16). He tells us that the Lord Jesus "received from God the Father honour and glory when such a voice came to Him from the Excellent Glory: 'This is My beloved Son, in

Whom I am well pleased'" (2 Peter 1:17). Peter was wide awake to the sufferings and glories of Christ.

On the third occasion when Peter slept, he was in prison, bound in chains between two soldiers and with two sentries at the door, on the eve of his planned execution. He was so soundly asleep the angel had to strike him to wake him up! Peter was the man who discovered his utter weakness when accused of being a disciple of Jesus. But in prison, he no longer rested on his own resources. Peter rested in Christ's love and the grace which kept him all the days of his of life. He was in the eye of a storm of persecution which cost the life of his dear friend James, but Peter slept under the wings of the Saviour he now trusted completely. I have no doubt James had the same experience.

Why does the Lord record these extraordinary events for us? He encourages us to know His love and grace in the storms of life and the peace of the One "under whose wings (we) have come for refuge" (Ruth 2:12).

Day 37

Thursday 23 April 2020

My witnesses

"But you shall receive power when the Holy Spirit has come upon you; and you shall be witnesses to Me in Jerusalem, and in all Judea and Samaria, and to the end of the earth."　　(Acts 1:8)

Immediately before the Lord Jesus returned to heaven, He focussed the hearts of His disciples on being witnesses to Him. He promised that this witness would extend to the end of the earth. Until Acts chapter 8, the young church was centred in Jerusalem and was blessed enormously by God. But gradually, issues began to arise. The first problem was covetousness, when Ananias and Sapphira pretended to give the full value of a property they sold to the service of God. Immediately before that happened, Barnabas provides an example of faithful sacrificial giving. Later, grumbling emerged over the distribution of funds to widows. God brings forward seven faithful men to address the problem. They included Stephen and Philip.

Stephen was a great witness to the Lord Jesus. It cost him his life and led to a great persecution (Acts 8:1). It seemed things were coming apart at the seams. But where were the disciples scattered? To the very places Jesus said they would be His witnesses: Judea and Samaria. Everywhere these ordinary saints of God went they preached the word of God (Acts 8:4).

Seven men were chosen, in the apostles' words, to "serve tables" (Acts 6:2). They included Stephen, the first martyr of the church, and Philip, the only man called an evangelist in the New Testament. I have often thought of how quickly the apostles overlooked the importance of serving tables. The Lord Jesus rose from a table to kneel and wash the feet of His disciples, to teach them to follow Him in lowly, loving and costly service. It was tables that Stephen and Philip were chosen to serve. I must never forget the example the Lord Jesus gave.

The Lord Jesus used the martyrdom of Stephen to fulfil His precise promise that His disciples would be His witnesses in Judea and Samaria. Philip was the man at the centre of the work of God in Samaria. God empowered him to preach Christ and perform miracles. As a result, the whole city rang with the joy of salvation. Amid this vast work, Philip was called by an angel of the Lord to go to Gaza, a desert place. To what purpose? So that in the impeccable timing of God, one influential man would be led to Christ by Philip and take the gospel into Ethiopia. Christ was beginning to take His witnesses to the end of the earth.

Let us pray always to be close to the Saviour. And let us also pray today that, through the witness of the ordinary lives of God's people and those gifted by Him in evangelism, the Lord Jesus will open hearts and fill them with the joy of salvation that filled Samaria and the heart of the Ethiopian eunuch.

Day 38

Friday 24 April 2020

Go tell (1)

He (Andrew) first found his own brother Simon.   *(John 1:41)*

Philip found Nathanael and said to him, "We have found Him of whom Moses in the law, and also the prophets, wrote—Jesus of Nazareth, the son of Joseph" (John 1:45). In these verses, the Lord Jesus teaches us about personal evangelism. Andrew and Peter were both fishermen by profession and Jesus called them to be fishers of men. Peter fished with a big net, so to speak, and drew thousands to the Lord. Andrew fished 'with a single line' and brought Peter and the boy with the loaves and fishes to Jesus. He also, with Philip, told Jesus about the Greeks who wanted to meet the Lord (John 12:20-22).

The Lord Jesus teaches us that the power to draw others to Christ comes from being in His presence. It is there we learn His love for us and His love for others. Sometimes as Christians we can talk a lot about what is wrong with the lives of other people and do not see what the Lord saw, people who are broken-hearted, blind, captive and lost. These were the people He came to save.

Andrew followed Jesus and spent the day with Him. Philip was found by Jesus with the words, "Follow me" (John 1:43). It is interesting that, in the final chapter of the Gospel of John, the Lord Jesus teaches us about fishing (evangelism), feeding (pastoral care) and following (discipleship). In the same chapter He finishes His conversation with Peter with the words, "You follow Me" (John 21:22). Peter's letters unfold the majesty of grace in a man who spent his life following the Saviour who loved him. He wrote in his final chapter, "The Lord is ... not willing that any should perish but that all should come to repentance" (2 Peter 3:9).

When I became a Christian, I was encouraged to share my faith in Christ. So I decided I would give out some gospel tracts. I was so nervous that, after posting the first tract, I ran away! I sometimes wonder if the Lord blessed that single leaflet. After being in the Lord's presence, it was the most natural thing for Andrew to tell his brother Peter and for Philip to tell his friend Nathaniel. Their witness was joyful, not fearful.

These friends also teach us to take the opportunities to witness first where we have the most influence. This is amongst our family and friends. This activity is not always easy. If Peter was ready to meet the Lord, Nathaniel was not! But Philip was not put off by Nathaniel's sarcasm about Nazareth. He doesn't enter into a theological debate with his friend. He says, "Come and see" (John 1:46). We often approach those we want to lead to Christ as if everything depended on our abilities to communicate and persuade. Salvation is God's work. Our work is to present the Lord Jesus and our experience of Him. The spiritual ability to do this work is only learnt in the presence of the One who came "to seek and save the lost" (Luke 19:10).

Day 39

Time to be a teapot

Now a certain woman named Lydia heard us. She was a seller of purple from the city of Thyatira, who worshipped God. The Lord opened her heart to heed the things spoken by Paul. And when she and her household were baptized, she begged us, saying, "If you have judged me to be faithful to the Lord, come to my house and stay." So she persuaded us. (Acts 16:14-15)

We have lived so long in a country blessed by Christianity that sometimes we almost speak as though it all started here. But Paul reminds us in his letter to the Ephesians that once we were "without Christ ... having no hope and without God in the world" (Ephesians 2:12). The day came when, by the direct guidance of the Holy Spirit of God, the Gospel arrived in Europe. How thankful we should be for that day! And it began in the heart of one woman, Lydia.

Paul and his fellow workers arrived in Philippi with the absolute assurance it was where God had placed them. This assurance gave them holy confidence in their service. But the Lord did not direct them to every place they visited in the city. No, they decided this by a daily faith. Their ministry began by finding a place where the Jews prayed at the riverside. They quickly connected with people at this meeting place. They didn't preach to the women they met, but, most naturally, engaged in conversation with them. Amongst these women was Lydia, a businesswoman from Thyatira and a proselyte. The Lord "opened her heart."

In John's Gospel chapter 4 the Lord went to Sychar's well to meet a woman of a different kind. She was not cultured or running a successful business, and her life was a mess. Nor do we know her name. But in gentle conversation the Lord opened her heart. Afterwards, He told His disciples, "Look at the fields, for they are already white for harvest!" (John 4:35). What did the Lord Jesus mean? He saw, in a world so damaged by sin, countless people who were ready to receive His salvation, but it needed His people to reach out with His love and grace.

During the lockdown, I have begun to reflect on how effectively I have followed the example of the Lord Jesus, of Andrew and Philip, of Paul, Silas and Timothy. It wasn't that they took opportunities to lead people to salvation. It was that they made such opportunities. Do I see "fields ... already white for harvest!"? Do I at least look for opportunities to present the Lord Jesus?

It is so encouraging to see how quickly Lydia enters into the fellowship of the Lord's people. She was so eager to provide her home as a base for Paul and his companions to continue their service.

The teapot is a remarkable thing. It only exists for two purposes: to receive from above and give to all around. The Lord poured His love into Lydia's opened heart, and, to display that love, He opened her home. He still does the same.

Day 40

Sunday 26 April 2020

Tell my Father

So you shall tell my father of all my glory.   *(Genesis 45:13)*

It is difficult to find a more compelling and complete illustration of the Lord Jesus in the Old Testament than that of Joseph. His story begins with the love that Jacob, his father, had for him and which he expressed in the gift of a coat of many colours. Woven into many features of the Tabernacle are the colours, white, blue, purple and scarlet. We see the glory of God in creation in its vast array of colours. The glory of God in salvation is seen in all the glorious 'colours' of the Lord Jesus, as God's Sovereign King, the Servant of God, the Son of Man and the Son of God.

Before we read of Joseph's sufferings, we are told both of Jacob's love for Joseph and of Joseph's future glory in Egypt, described in his dreams in Genesis 37. But the time came when the father Jacob sent Joseph, his son, to his brothers in Shechem. When Joseph arrived, his brothers had moved on. Someone asked Joseph what he wanted. He gave a simple answer, "I am looking for my brethren". These few words illustrate the experience of the Lord Jesus in this world: "He came to His own and His own did not receive Him" (John 1:11). Joseph's brothers conspired to kill him. But instead they sold him to Ishmaelite traders. The Lord Jesus was sold by Judas. He was not crucified by the Jews but handed over to the Romans to be nailed to the cross. Joseph sufferings ended in prison in Egypt. The Lord's suffering ended in death. Pharaoh brought Joseph out of prison to save his family and the nation of Egypt. The God of peace brought the Lord Jesus out of death as the great shepherd of the sheep (Hebrews 13:20). Pharaoh honoured Joseph with the gift of his signet ring. He was dressed in fine linen. Pharaoh placed a gold chain around Joseph's neck, and when he travelled in Pharaoh's chariot, they cried, "Bow the knee." The Lord Jesus ascended to heaven in glory, and one glorious day every knee shall bow and every tongue confess that Jesus is Lord to the glory of God the Father (see Philippians 2:10-11).

When Joseph was in prison, he interpreted the Cupbearer's dream to foretell the man's return to his position before Pharaoh. Afterwards, he said to the Cupbearer, "Only remember me, when it is well with you" (Genesis 40:14, ESV). After Joseph revealed himself to his brothers and assured them of salvation and safety in a new land, he says to them, "tell my father of all my glory in Egypt" (Genesis 45:13). This morning the Lord Jesus looks down upon His people in this world which He made and where He lived, suffered and died. It was here, too, that His glorious resurrection took place and from where heaven received Him in glory. He looks down with the desire He expressed, as the cross approached, in two powerful words, "Remember Me." He has made it well for us, and now He asks us to think about Him. Joseph told his brothers, as they returned to Jacob to bring him to Egypt, to tell his father of all his glory. The Father spoke from heaven about His beloved Son. His Father is now our Father. And we are brought into His presence to speak from earth to heaven of the glory of His Son. Let us not be quiet.

Day 41

The sight of God

And the Lord turned and looked at Peter. (Luke 22:61)

Over the past years social media has exploded: Facebook, WhatsApp, Twitter, Instagram, and now Zoom. Images and words can be flashed around the world instantaneously. There are two sides to this phenomenon. The first is the pleasure people get from sharing with others what they want others to see and hear. The second is the terror of people being scammed and victimised by those using the internet with evil intent. And, behind it all, is an industry accumulating a vast and complex store of information about individuals, families, communities and nations. It is an unsettling mixture of the known and the unknown in the hands of people we cannot see.

But what about being in the sight of God? God sees everything. His sight is not confined to the external but includes the thoughts and intents of our hearts and minds. God is both all-seeing and all-knowing. He sees and knows His entire creation, past, present and future – simultaneously. What God sees is far more sobering than the limited view of the information czars of this world.

Two statements embrace Peter's relationship with the Lord before His resurrection. The first is in John 1:42 where Andrew brought Peter to Jesus and Jesus "looked at him." The second is in Luke 22:60-61: "Immediately, while he was still speaking, the cock crowed. And the Lord turned and looked at Peter."

In that most profound moment we see what it means to be in the sight of God. We understand the Lord's complete knowledge of what we are by nature and where that takes us. And at the same moment, we see the depth of His love for us. As the Saviour is enduring the sufferings which led to Calvary, He shows in a look that we are always in His heart.

Many years ago a well-known and godly brother held a high position in the Bank of England. An issue about fraudulent practice arose in his department. The auditors, who had great respect for the brother and his Christian testimony, said to him, "You are above reproach." He replied, "If God projected my life onto that wall, I would have to leave this room in complete shame." The brother knew what it was to live in the sight of God.

The Lord loved us when He saw us in our greatest need, before we ever saw our need of Him. The Lord still sees our failures and frailties through the same eyes of love. He always looks upon us with a grace that lifts us to where He wants us to be. I could spend a lot of time and effort selecting and editing the images I want the world to see. But I need to spend far more time consciously living in the light and grace of the sight of God, being transformed into the image of His Son and my Saviour, the Lord Jesus.

Day 42

Tuesday 28 April 2020

Go tell (2)

"Go home to your friends, and tell them what great things the Lord has done for you, and how He has had compassion on you."

(Mark 5:19)

A few days ago we looked at the personal evangelism of Andrew and Philip. These ordinary men were not brought to Jesus by the evidence of His miraculous power. They met Him, and He transformed their lives.

Legion, the man the Lord spoke to in today's reading, was so different. There was probably a time when he lived an ordinary life. But when he met Jesus, he was engulfed by evil. Some commentators have suggested that it was Satan who caused the storm which oppressed the boat in which Jesus travelled to the country of the Gadarenes. They base their thinking on Satan's power described at the beginning of the book of Job. They suggest Satan was trying to protect what belonged to him, the man known as Legion. But Mark does not comment.

Mark tells us that Legion lived amongst the dead. He was uncontrollable and in constant mental and physical pain. When he sees Jesus afar off, he runs to Him in a turmoil of need and struggling under the power of the evil spirits which possessed him. Demonic forces are far more aware of the power of Christ than humans. This story teaches us what James writes, "You believe that there is one God. You do well. Even the demons believe—and tremble!" (James 2:19). The Lord Jesus has the power to command legions of angels, and He also has the power to defeat the legions of demons. He set Legion free.

Legion's transformation is one of the most beautiful descriptions of salvation. It illustrates so powerfully what Paul said in Acts 26:18: "to turn them from darkness to light, and from the power of Satan to God, that they may receive forgiveness of sins and an inheritance among those who are sanctified by faith in Me". Legion is described as "sitting and clothed and in his right mind" (Mark 5:15). Where there was death, demons and deep distress, there was a peace which passes all understanding and a heart that desired the constant presence of the Lord.

We must never forget the power and compassion Jesus had to redeem us. It is the same power and compassion He has to keep us day by day. He wants us to know and enjoy His peace (Philippians 4:7); to know we are clothed in His righteousness (Luke 15:22, Romans 3:21-22), and to have the mind of Christ (Philippians 2:5).

Legion was equipped and sent by the Lord on a mission, "Go home to your friends, and tell them what great things the Lord has done for you, and how He has had compassion on you."

Whether an Andrew, Philip, Martha, Mary or Legion, we all have our story to tell. May the Lord Jesus empower us to "Go tell."

Day 43

Wednesday 29 April 2020

The upper and lower springs

Caleb gave her the upper springs and the lower springs. (Judges 1:15)

As a young man, I worked in local government for the department responsible for clearing the city centre pavements of snow in the wintertime. When it snowed heavily, I had to turn up very early in the morning to help organise this work. I remember leaving my home one day after it had snowed through the night. It was the most beautiful cloudless morning. The stars shone brightly in the dark sky, especially the North Star. An untouched carpet of deep snow covered the avenue where we lived. There was not a soul about. Most of all, I remember the exhilaration of being the first person to walk through the fresh snow to work. I didn't feel the cold. I just felt alive!

This simple experience has often reminded of me of the wonder of each day that God gives to us. We live in a dark world, but we can start each day by looking up to the One who is the Bright and Morning Star with hope in our hearts. We can walk by faith day by day through all the experiences of life with the assurance that our times are in His hand. There is also a path which is uniquely ours. In these paths of righteousness, we learn the ways of God. Behind us, we leave footsteps. Some are joyful, and others are not. In front, we have yet to make footsteps. Each morning June and I pray that the Lord would go before us guiding our steps in the ordinary and extraordinary circumstances of life.

Caleb was a remarkable man of God. He had seen the Promised Land as one of the twelve spies. When the people feared to take possession of what God had promised them, he said to them,

"Let us go up at once and take possession, for we are well able to overcome it" (Numbers 13:30). But instead of possessing what God wanted to give them, their unbelief led them to endure nearly 40 years in the wilderness. But Caleb had seen the land and its beauty remained in his heart. When as an old man he entered the Promised Land, he spoke to his friend Joshua of how the Lord had kept him alive, and added, "Here I am this day, eighty-five years old. As yet I am as strong this day as on the day that Moses sent me; just as my strength was then, so now is my strength for war, both for going out and for coming in" (Joshua 14:10-11). The wilderness years were a very testing time. But Caleb had not lived them in bitterness and disappointment. He had walked before God in anticipation of what was to come.

When God gave Caleb his inheritance, his daughter, Achsah, came to her father to ask for the blessing of springs of water. In generous response, Caleb gave Achsah the upper springs and the lower springs (Judges 1:14-15). This gift reminds me of how God provides His word to bless and keep us in our experience of abundance (the upper springs) and of need (the lower springs). Caleb knew these experiences, and he wanted his children to know God's faithfulness throughout their lives too.

Paul writes, "Not that I speak in regard to need, for I have learned in whatever state I am, to be content: I know how to be abased, and I know how to abound. Everywhere and in all things I have learned both to be full and to be hungry, both to abound and to suffer need. I can do all things through Christ who strengthens me" (Philippians 4:11-13).

Let us open the door of this morning and know the exhilaration of our life in Christ.

Day 44

Forgiving one another

Let all bitterness, wrath, anger, clamour, and evil speaking be put away from you, with all malice. And be kind to one another, tender-hearted, forgiving one another, even as God in Christ forgave you.

(Ephesians 4:31-32)

A long time ago I fell out with a much older sister in our local fellowship. Today I can't remember why this happened, only the distress it caused. Around the same time we had invited a brother to come to our meeting to minister God's word. He didn't travel widely but he agreed to come. In the evening he spoke on Ephesians 4:31-32.

On that occasion in a small hall with not many people in attendance God taught me some very important lessons. He taught that He is mindful of the times that His people hurt each other and the damage this causes, not only to those involved, but also to the flock of God. He taught me, too, that He acts, when we won't, to bring about reconciliation between those who love each other in Christ, but whose relationship is damaged. He taught me that He can put His word into the hearts of those who serve Him, to bring about blessings they may never know about until they get to heaven. He taught me about the incisive power of God's word and how that power is so often expressed in the gentlest of ways. And the Lord Jesus taught me about the need to respond to what He asks us to do.

At the end of the meeting I sat overwhelmed by the need to be reconciled to a dear sister I loved in the Lord. I got up and went to her and began to speak. But she stopped me and said, "Gordon, I want to say sorry for what happened between us."

In that moment we both had the most wonderful sense of the joy and blessing of the kindness, tenderness and forgiveness of God expressed in the Person of Christ.

From the beginning of creation Satan's work has been to destroy our relationship with God and with each other. He did this in the lives of Adam and Eve and in the lives of their children, Cain and Abel. He did it in the families of the patriarchs and in the nation of Israel and he has continued to do it throughout the course of the history of this sad world. Most distressingly, he has done it amongst the flock of God.

The Lord Jesus, before He went to the cross, prayed to the Father, "And the glory which You gave Me I have given them, that they may be one just as We are one: I in them, and You in Me; that they may be made perfect in one, and that the world may know that You have sent Me, and have loved them as You have loved Me" (John 17:22-23). It is the love of God for us, and its expression through us, that benefits the flock of God so much and speaks so powerfully to the world. I damage the fellowship of God's people and their witness to the world by being unkind, hard-hearted, and unforgiving. The remedy, as always, is found in the Person of the Lord Jesus and having the courage and humility to follow Him.

Day 45

Friday 01 May 2020

Walking into desks

Now when they came to Marah, they could not drink the waters of Marah, for they were bitter. Therefore the name of it was called Marah. And the people complained against Moses, saying, "What shall we drink?" So he cried out to the Lord, and the Lord showed him a tree. When he cast it into the waters, the waters were made sweet.   *(Exodus 15:23-25)*

The majority of Exodus 15 is a hymn of praise to God for bringing the children of Israel through the Red Sea in the most incredible act of salvation. We have the song of Moses and the people, and the song of Miriam. I doubt there has ever been such a vast choir worshipping God so joyously. It is an amazing scene of a nation responding as one to the God of their salvation. Then we come to the waters of Marah.

Within days the beautiful songs of praise had ended. Instead, the same people became a grumbling mass, focusing their displeasure upon the man God chose to lead them into salvation. There is an irrationality about their unbelief. They did not stop to consider for a moment their experience of the power of God's love for them. Nor did they consider that it was the same God who had now led them into the Wilderness of Shur, and to Marah's bitter waters. It was in this wilderness, in Genesis 16, that Hagar discovered that God saw her and cared for her. How quickly I can lose faith when tested by the circumstances of life! I have often made the mistake of thinking, or at least acting, as though such circumstances happened by chance and that there was no purpose of God in them.

At work, I once left the drawer of my desk open. Later, as a consequence, I walked into it and hurt my shin. I remember thinking what possible purpose that event had other than to teach me to be more careful. Sometime later, a colleague had a similar experience. I cannot share with you the words that came out of his mouth. But it helped me to understand that God allows us to go through circumstances small and great to make us into the people He wants us to be.

It was not by chance the people were at the waters of Marah. It was to teach them at the beginning of the wilderness journey, and in view of all that they would face, that God would bring blessing out of bitterness. We see this in the stories of men like Jacob and Joseph, and women like Ruth and Hannah. But how did the waters become sweet? By Moses seeing and casting a tree into them. Later, at the end of verse 26, God says, "I am the Lord, your healer" (ESV). It is hard not to think of another tree we are aware of when we read what Moses did. Peter writes about the Lord Jesus, "He Himself bore our sins in His body on the tree, that we might die to sin and live to righteousness. By His wounds you have been healed" (1 Peter 2:24, ESV).

We are saved by the love of Christ seen in all its fullness at Calvary. This love teaches us to defeat sin and guides our steps in paths of righteousness. Its healing power presides over our lives. And, in verse 27, that same love leads us to enjoy all the blessings of God in a hostile world, foretold in the oasis that was Elim.

Day 46

Saturday 02 May 2020

Abide in Me

"Abide in Me, and I in you. As the branch cannot bear fruit of itself, unless it abides in the vine, neither can you, unless you abide in Me."
(John 15:4)

At the beginning of the Bible, God takes just two chapters to outline His astonishing work of Creation. The most brilliant minds in science continue to be mesmerised by its mysteries. It takes God ten chapters at the end of Exodus to describe in the smallest detail the building of the Tabernacle. God begins this process with the words, "Let them make Me a sanctuary, that I may dwell among them" (Exodus 25:8). Moses finished the construction of this small structure in the final chapter of Exodus, where we read, "the glory of the Lord filled the tabernacle" (Exodus 40:35). At the end of the Bible, in Revelation 21, we read, "Behold, the tabernacle of God is with men, and He will dwell with them, and they shall be His people. God Himself will be with them and be their God. And God will wipe away every tear from their eyes; there shall be no more death, nor sorrow, nor crying. There shall be no more pain, for the former things have passed away" (verses 3-4).

In March this year, the world began to stop. The engines which drive the world's economy fell silent. The crowded cities emptied, and everything became still. We were in a place we had never been in before. Many of us alone. We began to understand our smallness.

I have never forgotten some ministry I listened to over twenty years ago by a brother who is still a dear friend. He spoke about Elijah raising the son of the widow of Zarephath in 1 Kings 17, emphasising the words, "And he (Elijah) stretched himself out on the child three times, and cried out to the Lord and said, 'O Lord my God, I pray, let this child's soul come back to him.' Then the Lord heard the voice of Elijah; and the soul of the child came back to him, and he revived" (verses 21-22). My friend said the prophet stretched himself to become small. He used this beautiful illustration to reflect on the grace of the Lord Jesus.

At the beginning of the New Testament, Matthew writes, "'Behold, the virgin shall be with child, and bear a Son, and they shall call His name Immanuel,' which is translated, 'God with us'" (Matthew 1:23).

I love to look up into the night sky to be amazed anew by the glory of God's immense creation. I love to look at the bush outside our lounge window and see the tiny birds that come there to feed. But what truly astonishes my heart is when I consider that the Saviour used His power to become small and to dwell amongst us so that we could live with Him. We will know the wonder of this in all the glory of a coming day.

But today the question is, are we responding to His invitation to abide in Him?

Day 47

Come near to me

And Joseph said to his brothers, "Please come near to me." So they came near. (Genesis 45:4)

In Genesis 48 we read, "Then Israel saw Joseph's sons, and said, 'Who are these?' Joseph said to his father, 'They are my sons, whom God has given me in this place.' And he said, 'Please bring them to me, and I will bless them.' Now the eyes of Israel were dim with age, so that he could not see. Then Joseph brought them near him, and he kissed them and embraced them" (Genesis 48:8-10).

The story of Jacob and Joseph ends as it had begun. It focuses upon the love between a father and his son. The journey which led to Joseph's glory in Egypt began because his father sent him to find his brothers. His obedience in travelling alone to find brothers he knew hated him was always going to be a dangerous journey. But was he alone? If I had been Joseph, perhaps I would have left my coat of many colours at home. Maybe I would have put on something ordinary so as not to alienate my siblings further. But not Joseph. He would not take off that which spoke of his father's love for him. We know what that cost him in the suffering and distance he experienced in the pit, at the hands of the Ishmaelites, in Potiphar's house and finally in prison.

But we have not read about distance, rather about nearness. Genesis 45:4 allows us to see love, so deep and forgiving, expressed by Joseph's words, "Please come near to me." The development of Christendom has erected so many things such as rituals, dress, buildings, altars, icons and endless divisions, which have succeeded in putting distance between God and

His children. And also, like Joseph's brothers, we can hesitate to come near because we remember our failure and unworthiness. Sadly, we can fail to understand and respond to the simplicity and overwhelming desire of the Lord Jesus to embrace us in His perfect love.

When Joseph goes to meet his father Jacob in Genesis 48, he does not go alone. We often think of that glorious day when the Lord Jesus will fulfil His promise to bring His own into the Father's house. When we meet young children that we know, we often ask with affection, "And who is this?" – not an expression of the need for an introduction, but of delight. Perhaps there will be a moment in heaven when the Father delights in asking the Son, "Whose are these?" And the Lord Jesus will reply, "The children that You gave Me." In that day, we shall know, and never cease to know, what it is to be fully embraced by the love of God.

Joseph brought Ephraim and Manasseh near to Jacob. In doing so, these children witnessed the love that existed between their father and grandfather. It was the basis of all their blessings. The Lord Jesus has brought us near to Himself and His Father. We see the glory of the love of the Father and the Son. It is the source of all our blessings, and today it appeals to us afresh, in the power of the blessed Holy Spirit, to come near and worship.

Day 48

Monday 04 May 2020

Lessons in isolation: Moses

Now the man Moses was very humble, more than all men who were on the face of the earth. (Numbers 12:3)

Our government is cautiously considering the country's pathway out of lockdown. This announcement has made me think about what God wants me to learn from the lockdown experience. Today is Day 50 of this period of isolation. It seems a long time. But I cannot think of anyone who endured isolation for as long as Moses.

Moses was born into isolation. Egypt had forgotten their great saviour Joseph. They had enslaved his people, and when Moses was born, they were butchering all newly born male children. Moses' isolation began before he could walk or talk, in a tiny basket floated on the River Nile. It continued for the next 40 years in the palaces of one of the world's greatest monarchs. Moses was a prince, and materially he had everything. But he was isolated from his people. When he visited his kin and discovered an Egyptian beating a Hebrew slave, he murdered the attacker to protect one of his people. This powerful prophetic act foretold the deliverance of the children of Israel and the judgement of Egypt. But it also resulted in Moses fleeing for his life and spending the next 40 years in far greater isolation from his people. Moses spent these years, not as a prince in a palace, but as a shepherd in the wilderness.

It is from the wilderness at Horeb, the mountain of God, that God calls Moses to lead His people out of slavery to the land He had promised to Abraham, Isaac and Jacob. For 80 years God had been preparing Moses for that day. And what was the result of all of God's 80 years of work in the life of Moses? He was "very humble, more than all men who were on the face of the earth" (Numbers 12:3). God had taken this powerful prince of Egypt, who had so much natural strength and confidence, and changed him into a lowly shepherd who would lead a nation into salvation and to the edge of the Promised Land.

I cannot count the times I have told the story of the lady who had a beautiful set of crockery. It was her pride and joy. She kept it in a display cabinet and, every Sunday, she took it out to clean the pieces. One day, she dropped the milk jug and broke it. She tried to repair it by gluing it together, but it didn't look as good as the other pieces. What could she do? She filled it with milk and used it every day. For God to make us useful and to honour Him, He has to humble us. But meekness is not weakness. Spiritually weak men don't lead nomadic nations for forty years and bring them to the border of their destination. No; humility is the way God transmits His power through our obedience and dependence upon Him.

God did not demonstrate His greatest power when He flung stars into space. We saw this power when our Saviour, Jesus Christ, stepped into the world He made. The same Jesus who said, "Take My yoke upon you, and learn of Me; for I am meek and lowly in heart" (Matthew 11:29, AV).

I hope 50 days of isolation has encouraged me to respond to the Lord's invitation to learn of Him.

Day 49

Lessons in isolation: Naomi and Ruth

Then the women said to Naomi, "Blessed be the Lord, who has not left you this day without a close relative; and may his name be famous in Israel! And may he be to you a restorer of life and a nourisher of your old age; for your daughter-in-law, who loves you, who is better to you than seven sons, has borne him."

(Ruth 4:14-15)

The story of the Book of Ruth is told within the framework of four decisions. Elimelech made the first decision. He left Bethlehem to escape the famine in Israel. This grave error of judgement cost him his life and that of his two sons. It made three women widows, and it left his wife, Naomi, alone and isolated in a foreign country.

Naomi made the second decision: to return home to Bethlehem. That decision revealed the complete devotion of her daughter-in-law, Ruth. There must have been something remarkable about the character and faith of Naomi. Ruth observed Naomi as she lived in a strange land and endured a life of intense sadness. It produced in Ruth love, faithfulness and a willingness to leave her country and her people. Ruth put herself into isolation in Israel to provide for Naomi.

The third decision was Ruth's determination to work: "Let me go into the field and glean" (Ruth 2:2). Her works expressed her faith. Her brightness and energy immediately attracted Boaz to her. He tells her she had come under the protection of the wings of the God of Israel (Ruth 2:12).

Boaz took the final decision. It was the decision to redeem Elimelech's land and to make Ruth his wife. God, in a remarkable display of grace, brought blessing out of the bitterness of the enforced isolation of Naomi and the willing isolation of Ruth. He formed a new family, blessed Naomi and prepared the way for the birth of Israel's greatest king, David. In doing so, He teaches us some valuable lessons about the pathway of faith.

Elimelech is a warning to us not to allow difficult circumstances to drive us away from the blessing of God. They should always lead us to the Throne of Grace. In the presence of God, a couple make a joint decision at the start of marriage. It is to be faithful to each other for the rest of their lives. To stay together, we should make every other decision in the same way.

Naomi teaches us it is never too late to return to the Lord and discover He can restore the years we think are wasted: "So I will restore to you the years that the swarming locust has eaten" (Joel 2:25). Ruth shows us that God always responds to our faith and desire to follow His will:

> "Trust in the Lord with all your heart,
> And lean not on your own understanding;
> In all your ways acknowledge Him,
> And He shall direct your paths.
> Do not be wise in your own eyes."
> (Proverbs 3:5-7)

Finally, Boaz illustrates that the Lord Jesus, our Redeemer, saves us and keeps us. We are brought beneath His mighty wings and nothing can isolate us from His love.

> "For I am persuaded that neither death nor life, nor angels nor principalities nor powers, nor things present nor things to come, nor height nor depth, nor any other created thing, shall be able to separate us from the love of God which is in Christ Jesus our Lord" (Romans 8:38-39).

Day 50

Wednesday 06 May 2020

Helps

And God has appointed these in the church: first apostles, second prophets, third teachers, after that miracles, then gifts of healings, helps, administrations, varieties of tongues. (1 Corinthians 12:28)

For several years June and I and friends produced a children's Christian magazine called *Helps*. We based the name of the magazine on a character called Help in John Bunyan's book *Pilgrim's Progress*. In the book it was Help who said to Christian, "Give me your hand" and pulled him out of the Slough of Despond.

In 1 Corinthians chapter 12 Paul lists foundational and extraordinary gifts given to the body of Christ. In the same list he includes helps. The word means to provide assistance. It seems such a simple and ordinary action, yet the apostle places it amongst the ministries which build and maintain the body of Christ. Luke chose a similar word in Acts 27:17 when the sailors used helps or cables to strengthen the hull of the ship when it was in danger. It described a nautical term called "frapping", and it means to hold something together tightly. It is an excellent illustration of the ability of those brothers and sisters in Christ who work tirelessly to encourage all the people of God, especially in times of crisis.

The dignity and value of helps are brought home to us when we see them demonstrated in the Lord Jesus. In Hebrews 4:15-16, we are told, "We do not have a High Priest who cannot sympathize with our weaknesses, but was in all points tempted as we are, yet without sin. Let us therefore come boldly to the throne of grace, that we may obtain mercy and find grace to help in time of need." The Lord Jesus sits on the Throne of Grace as the Helper. In Hebrews 13:6, the writer quotes from Psalm 118:6 – "The Lord is my Helper." It has the sense of 'standing by our side'. Paul witnessed it first when he heard Stephen, before he was stoned to death, describing Jesus standing at the right hand of God and alongside His faithful servant. And Paul experienced it himself. He remembers a time when everyone forsook him, but then wrote "The Lord stood by me" (2 Timothy 4:17).

The Lord Jesus refers in John 14 to the Holy Spirit as "another Helper". He describes someone just like Himself, "And I will pray the Father, and He will give you another Helper, that He may abide with you for ever, even the Spirit of truth" (verses 16-17). It is through this Helper that the Lord is in us.

We see this ministry of help in Jehovah in the Old Testament. And in the New Testament we see it is a ministry which occupies the Lord Jesus in heaven and the Holy Spirit on earth. Some believers are given by God that wonderful gift of being helps. But the Lord Jesus also encourages every one of us, as members of His body, to help one another. He teaches us to be sensitive to the needs of others and to draw alongside when needed. He helps us to act in love. These actions are often simple, and expressed by a hand on the shoulder, a word of encouragement, a visit, a letter, an email, a telephone call, a gift and, of course, in prayer. He makes us into a people who are always outward-looking, understanding, kindly and seeking the welfare of others. He teaches us to follow His example and to go about doing good (Acts 10:38). He aims to make us like Himself.

Day 51

Thursday 07 May 2020

Thankfulness

And one of them, when he saw that he was healed, returned, and with a loud voice glorified God, and fell down on his face at His feet, giving Him thanks. And he was a Samaritan. (Luke 17:15-16)

I remember as a young Christian reading George Whitefield's *Journals*. He was an Anglican who became one of the key figures of the Methodist movement and a remarkable evangelist. God used him extensively here and in the United States. Whitfield wrote that, whenever he returned to Oxford University, he would run to the field where he had knelt before God and opened his heart to Christ. In that field he would pour out his heart in thankfulness to God for his salvation.

You can understand the ten lepers being overcome by joy at their miraculous healing. But only one turned back to praise God and to fall at the feet of the Lord Jesus to say thank you. It made the Lord sad that the nine forgot to thank God, but He was thankful the Samaritan had not.

Ingratitude should never mark the people of God. Paul always expresses thankfulness as he writes to the early Christians. He lifts his heart in constant gratitude to God for the Ephesian church (Ephesians 1:16). Paul expresses thankfulness to the Philippians for their help and support when in distress, and when other churches did not help him (Philippians 4:14-15). And he encourages the Colossian believers to be characterised by a spirit of thankfulness, "And let the peace of God rule in your hearts, to which also you were called in one body; and be thankful" (Colossians 3:15). Luke records, after being shipwrecked with Paul, the unusual kindness of the people of Malta towards them in Acts 28:1-2.

But above all it is the example of the thankfulness of the Lord Jesus which touches our hearts. He rejoiced in the Spirit and thanked His Father for revealing His truths to the disciples (Luke 10:21). John records the Lord giving thanks for the five barley loaves and two small fish in John 6:11 and refers to it again in verse 23. At the grave of Lazarus, Jesus lifts His eyes to heaven to thank the Father (John 11:41). And we see the thankfulness of the Lord powerfully expressed on the Passover night and at the institution of the Lord's supper (Luke 22:19). The Lord Jesus' thankfulness relates to our spiritual blessing, our daily food, our new life, and our response of remembrance and worship. It is humbling to think of the Lord of Glory and the Lord of All expressing thankfulness. What a joy it must have been to His heart when the healed Samaritan fell at His feet to say thank you!

I regret as a young man not expressing as I should have my thanks to the many saints who were so kind to me. As I have grown older, I look back with appreciation to God for the countless times His people displayed His goodness and for His provision every day of my life. And I try to take the opportunity where I can to remember with thankfulness what I took for granted in the past.

> It is good to give thanks to the Lord,
> And to sing praises to Your name, O Most High;
> To declare Your lovingkindness in the morning,
> And Your faithfulness every night.
> (Psalm 92:1-2)

Day 52

Friday 08 May 2020

Good News

This day is a day of good news, and we remain silent.   (2 Kings 7:9)

Tuesday 08 May 1945 was the day the Allied Forces accepted the unconditional surrender of Nazi Germany's armed forces. The day is now celebrated as Victory in Europe Day and popularly known as VE Day in the UK. To gain that victory, just under a year before on 06 June 1944, the Allied Forces landed on the Normandy beaches in France. Those forces included soldiers from all over the world, many fighting for their occupied countries. Amongst them were Polish soldiers, whose country was the first to be invaded. In preparation for D-Day, as 6th June 1944 became known, some of those Polish soldiers were in barracks in Scotland. A young Christian felt exercised to share the gospel with these young men, many of whom would sacrifice their lives in the coming conflict. He managed to get hold of some gospel tracts in Polish and permission to distribute them to the soldiers. He could not speak Polish, and many soldiers had little knowledge of English, but they appreciated his visit and took the tracts. They never saw each other again.

Many years later, in the emerging freedoms which led up to the fall of Communism in Eastern Europe, a brother from Scotland visited Christians in Poland. They took him to hear a Polish evangelist whose ministry had led a vast number of people to Christ. During the meeting the evangelist told the story of his conversion. He was one of the young Polish soldiers in the barracks in Scotland all those years before. He recalled a young man spending time with him and giving him a small tract in his language. He explained how that meeting and that tract led him to trust in the Lord Jesus on the eve of D-Day.

Today we will remember the horrors of war and the day when peace came at such an enormous cost. People will think about the sacrifice of loved ones to end that dreadful conflict. And we will be thankful for the freedoms we now enjoy. We do this while experiencing another crisis which is so costly.

Each Lord's Day, we remember the day when the Lord Jesus died. As the Good Shepherd, He stood "between us and foe, and willingly died in our stead." We remember His victory cry, "It is finished" and rejoice in the triumph of His resurrection – "He is risen!" By faith in the Lord Jesus, we have peace with God and know the Prince of peace and the God of peace. We experience God's love, walk by faith and have a glorious hope in Christ.

In 2 Kings chapter 7 God miraculously scattered the Syrian armies besieging Samaria. Four lepers were the first to discover this and enjoyed the spoils of war. But then they stopped and said to each other, "This day is a day of good news, and we remain silent" (verse 9). Immediately they began to spread the good news. One young man led another young man to Christ. That witness led to a great number of people in another country trusting in Christ. It is the goodness of God and the majesty of His grace that challenges us to share the Gospel, no matter how falteringly, and to trust God to do the miraculous.

Day 53

Victorious faith

"If only my master were with the prophet who is in Samaria! For he would heal him of his leprosy." (2 Kings 5:3)

I have been frustrated by the poor quality of my internet service recently. I spent an hour on the phone with several customer service advisors trying to sort things out and complaining about the failures of their product. We all like to complain at times and share experiences of being poorly treated.

Imagine being taken as a very young person from your family, your town, your country and made a slave in a strange land. Think of the experience: many bitter tears, endless regret, hatred for those who had forced you into such a life, and doubt that God cared for you.

Naaman's story, like those of Rahab and Ruth, shines like a bright star witnessing to the glory of the grace of God. But how did this gifted general, leprous as he was, come to know God's kindness? God blessed him through a nameless child whom Naaman had made a slave. The story of Naaman is a beautiful record of God's salvation and an astonishing demonstration of God's power through a child's love, faith and hope.

The young girl practised what the Lord Jesus taught hundreds of years later:

> "You have heard that it was said, 'You shall love your neighbour and hate your enemy.' But I say to you, love your enemies, bless those who curse you, do good to those who hate you, and pray for

those who spitefully use you and persecute you" (Matthew 5:43-44).

Jesus also refers to the story in Luke 4:27, "And many lepers were in Israel in the time of Elisha the prophet, and none of them was cleansed except Naaman the Syrian."

The little servant expressed faith in adverse circumstances and apparent powerlessness. She promised something which had not happened before. It wasn't a timid witness but a very bold one, "If only my master were with the prophet who is in Samaria! For he would heal him of his leprosy." Notice how she addressed Naaman as "my master". She teaches us that she had accepted her life under the hand of God. But that acceptance did not subdue her faith: it became the base upon which she witnessed powerfully to the God of all grace. She was not diminished by complaint. She didn't ask, as even Joseph did to the cupbearer, "When it is well with you remember me" (Genesis 40:14). This remarkable child desired the salvation of the man who had robbed her of everything.

Time and time again, God teaches us of the power of a life of faith which refuses to be crushed by circumstances, but sees them as the battleground on which love, faith and hope are victorious. Interestingly, it was a complaining spirit that nearly robbed Naaman of the blessing of God. In furious pride, he said, "Are not the Abanah and the Pharpar, the rivers of Damascus, better than all the waters of Israel? Could I not wash in them and be clean?" (2 Kings 5:12). It was the humility and gentle appeal of his servants that led him into Jordan and a new life.

As a new day stretches before us, may God give us the grace to live victoriously: "But thanks be to God, who gives us the victory through our Lord Jesus Christ. Therefore, my beloved brethren, be steadfast, immovable, always abounding in the work of the Lord, knowing that your labour is not in vain in the Lord" (1 Corinthians 15:57-58).

Day 54

Sunday 10 May 2020

Believe in Me

"My Lord and my God!" (John 20:28)

We all have our journey of faith. No matter how far we are along that journey, there are constant reminders of our weakness. But it is on that same journey that we learn the power of the love and grace of the Lord Jesus. Thomas never seemed the happiest of men. In the story of Lazarus, he speaks about going to die. He could see only the darkness of death, but then witnessed the light of life in the Lord Jesus, as the resurrection and the life. In the upper room, in John 14, the Lord Jesus encourages His disciples not to be troubled but to believe in Him. He was going to heaven, and one glorious day He would bring His own into the Father's house. He had told them several times that this meant He had to go into death at the cross of Calvary. But Thomas says to the Lord that the disciples did not know where He was going so could not know the way. Jesus gave the wonderful answer, "I am the way, the truth, and the life. No one comes to the Father except through Me" (John 14:6).

The Bible does not tell us why Thomas was not with his friends when the risen Jesus came to His disciples in John 20. With joy in their hearts, the disciples tell Thomas that they had seen the Lord. For three years Thomas had been with the Lord Jesus, hearing His word and seeing His power. He had heard the Lord Jesus speak about His suffering, death and resurrection. He had been there when Jesus raised Lazarus. The men he had lived with during that time, friends Thomas loved and trusted, told him they had seen the Lord. At that moment, Thomas had a unique opportunity to answer to the Lord's words in John 14:1,

"Believe in Me." Instead, he says, "Unless I see in His hands the print of the nails, and put my finger into the print of the nails, and put my hand into His side, I will not believe" (John 20:25).

Eight days later Jesus appears to His disciples again and, standing amongst them, says, "Peace to you!" Then, in the most astonishing act of grace, He invites Thomas to do what his wilful unbelief demanded and at the same time to fulfil what the Lord's love demanded: "Believe in Me". It brought from dear Thomas' heart utter worship: "My Lord and my God!"

The Lord, and only the Lord, rebukes Thomas for his unbelief. At the same time, He looked forward to the worship of the millions of saints who would never see what Thomas saw but who would believe in the Saviour who died and rose again for them. The risen Saviour, as the Great Shepherd, brought two men back to Himself: Thomas, who denied Him in resurrection, and Peter, who denied Him as He suffered. The love of Christ conquers our most profound failings and makes us, first like Thomas, into worshippers – "My Lord and my God", and then like Peter, into followers – "You follow Me" (John 21:22).

> "That the genuineness of your faith, being much more precious than gold that perishes, though it is tested by fire, may be found to praise, honour, and glory at the revelation of Jesus Christ, whom having not seen you love. Though now you do not see Him, yet believing, you rejoice with joy inexpressible and full of glory, receiving the end of your faith—the salvation of your souls" (1 Peter 1:7-9).

Day 55

Monday 11 May 2020

Power for obedience

"This is My beloved Son. Hear Him!" (Luke 9:35)

Usually, Monday mornings are the start of the new working week. Our minds can be full of all kinds of things we have to do. I remember staying with a brother who had been a missionary in the West Indies. He said to me, "I don't like my children to tumble into the day." I have often thought of his words and the times I have tumbled into the day. Mondays can be the day when the demands and responsibilities of life engulf us, and activity sweeps us through another week.

As we remembered the Lord yesterday, I found myself reflecting on the three special moments in the Bible when the Father speaks of His delight in His Son. The first is at the baptism of the Lord Jesus in Luke 3:22, as His public ministry in divine love and holy energy was about to begin. As Jesus came out of the River Jordan, the Father expressed His delight in His Son's obedience in love to do the work the Father had given Him to do. He not only delighted in it at that moment but also in the thirty years that led up to it, and all the Son would accomplish from that moment to the glory of God the Father.

The second occasion was on the Mount of Transfiguration when Peter, James and John saw the glory of Jesus and also saw Moses and Elijah speaking with Him. These two men represent the Law and the Prophets which foretold the sufferings and glory of the Saviour. Luke tells us they spoke with the Lord of His suffering and death that Jesus was about to accomplish at Jerusalem. Moses never entered the Promised Land. Instead, God personally showed it to him from Mount

Nebo (Deuteronomy 34:1). But there was Moses on the Mount of Transfiguration. Grace takes us where the law never could. Elijah, who like Enoch did not die, was there as well. Moses and Elijah remind us of the dead in Christ and also the saints who are alive when the Lord comes again. He will take us into His glorious presence (1 Thessalonians 4). The Father closes the scene with the words, "This is My beloved Son. Hear Him!", and afterwards they only saw Jesus. Here the Father is teaching us that communion with Christ is the power for our obedience.

In John 12, after Philip and Andrew tell Jesus about the Greeks who wanted to see Him, the Lord says in verse 24, "Unless a grain of wheat falls into the ground and dies, it remains alone; but if it dies, it produces much grain." The verse is about the cross, and the subsequent joy that lay before the Lord. The Greeks who wanted to see the Lord were in a nation which had rejected the same Lord. They were a token of that vast company the lonely death of our Saviour would bring into being; the "much grain". But then the Lord measures that loneliness, "Now My soul is troubled, and what shall I say? 'Father, save Me from this hour'? But for this purpose I came to this hour. Father, glorify Your name." The Father's responds "I have both glorified it and will glorify it again" (verses 27-28).

These brief holy glimpses allow us to see the pleasure the Father has in the obedience of His beloved Son. That obedience expressed His love for the Father and His love for us. It is only enjoyed as we, like Peter, James and John, are taken up into His presence day by day. There we learn to listen to the Lord and find our life, not engulfed by busyness, but embraced by the calmness of His presence and enriched by the spiritual fruitfulness it produces (John 15).

Day 56

Tuesday 12 May 2020

The joy of God

Then all the tax collectors and the sinners drew near to Him to hear Him.

(Luke 15:1)

A young girl who lost her parents was taken into care in a Christian orphanage in the countryside. They cared for her well, but it was a strict home, and the girl was very lonely and unhappy there. One day she decided she would run away. She found herself beside the gate of a field. An old donkey strolled towards her and nestled its head against her shoulder. The young girl stroked its face and said to her new friend, "You must be a Christian; you have such a long face!"

It is difficult to think of a more joyful chapter than Luke 15. And it originates from the heart of the Lord Jesus. We should never forget that the Lord Jesus became the Man of sorrows for our redemption. He is not the Man of sorrows now. He is our risen glorious Lord and Head. And during His suffering ministry, He brought the joy of healing, forgiveness and salvation to so many broken lives. It was during that ministry that He spoke of the joy of God.

In Luke 15, the Lord describes His joy as the Good Shepherd finding the lost sheep. This parable was not just a picture. It was the Lord's experience when He encountered Legion, Zacchaeus and the repentant dying thief. He describes the Holy Spirit's joy in the simple story of a woman with a lamp searching for a valuable lost coin. Down the centuries, the Holy Spirit has searched in this dark world with the Word of God, to find valuable souls and rejoice in their salvation. And finally, the Lord Jesus describes the joy of God the Father's heart as His love embraces us, covers us in the righteousness of Christ and brings us into the family of God.

But what prompted this overwhelming expression of the joy of God? It was when those in the most profound spiritual need drew near to Jesus to hear Him. Why would those who were so far from God want to come so close? The Lord Jesus was the most approachable Person. No matter how deeply people felt their unworthiness, they wanted to be near Jesus. The Lord did not need, like the High Priest in Exodus 28, to have a signet upon His head saying, "Holiness to the Lord" (vers 36). He was holy. And when Jesus was on earth, God was not in the cloud, or on a mountain top or behind a thick curtain in an imposing temple, He was here in all the power and beauty of holiness. But His holy presence did not drive away unholy people. It drew them near. They did not come out of curiosity; they came like Mary to hear His words of grace. They listened as the Lord told them of the joy God would have when they opened their hearts to His love and forgiveness. I wonder how many tax collectors and sinners who were led to Christ that day later became part of the early Church?

Moses' face shone after being in the presence of God. Stephen had a face like the face of an angel when he witnessed to his people. God wants our faces to shine too.

> "But we all, with unveiled face, beholding as in a mirror the glory of the Lord, are being transformed into the same image from glory to glory, just as by the Spirit of the Lord" (2 Corinthians 3:18).

> "For it is the God who commanded light to shine out of darkness, who has shone in our hearts to give the light of the knowledge of the glory of God in the face of Jesus Christ" (2 Corinthians 4:6).

Day 57

Wednesday 13 May 2020

A brother

Erastus, the treasurer of the city, greets you, and Quartus, a brother. (Romans 16:23)

I first came amongst Christians as a child when, along with my two sisters, I went to Sunday School. As the eldest, I led the three of us into a big old building, which I still remember with great affection. The first person I met was an older man with a kindly face who welcomed us at the door. Over the coming years, he was a brother who by his simple faithfulness and quiet, cheerful ways taught me about following the Saviour. He was a farmer, who lived further away from the meeting than anyone else. But he was first at the meeting. This was not out of ritual, but because it was a joy to be there. He and his dear wife had no children, but he always engaged with the young people. I never heard him preach the gospel, minister the word or pray in the meeting. The only time I heard his voice was when he gave out J.G. Deck's beautiful hymn, "Lord we are Thine." He always chose this hymn. And I think of it as being his legacy to me. It expressed this delightful brother's gratitude to God for his salvation and the life he had in Christ. It recorded his joy that the Lord loved him, his desire to live by faith for the Lord, and the living hope he had in the Lord. The words remind me of the man.

As a farmer he was very practical, always cheerfully doing simple and sometimes complex things to help the Lord's people. He built the heater which warmed the water when we had a baptism. Every August Bank Holiday he and his wife would invite the assembly to his farm. When they retired, they also invited us to their bungalow, and he arranged for us to play games on the field behind his home.

One day the young people in the meeting had the bright idea to rent an allotment so that they could grow vegetables and distribute them to local older people. So we did. Of course, we knew nothing about allotments or vegetables. But we knew a man who did. And this dear old brother came to the fallow piece of earth which was our allotment, lent us gardening tools and showed us what to do. And we grew vegetables. I wrote to the council and asked them for the addresses of older people who lived in the area, explaining our idea (not something that you could do today!). The council sent me a list of names and addresses and so began a ministry towards the older people who lived in the area. Everyone worked together, making cards, cooking meals at Christmas and arranging a trip to the seaside to share the gospel with our new friends. The Lord blessed the exercise.

I have valued so much over the years the features of Christ expressed in the practical and joyful lives of ordinary believers. In Romans 16:23 Paul refers to two men in the same verse. The first was Erastus, a man who held high public office and must have been very well known. Paul delights in mentioning how God saves such notable and able men. He does not do this to impress us with their ability but with the grace of God. This grace is able to reach men in high places, where their pride and self-assurance often separates them from the love of Christ. Paul refers to this in 1 Corinthians 1:26, "For you see your calling, brethren, that not many wise according to the flesh, not many mighty, not many noble, are called." We should pray for such people today.

Paul then refers to Quartus, a brother. He does not need to write more. But the descriptions Paul uses in this short verse challenge us about what we value. We, like Samuel, can admire people who are head and shoulders above others. But God looks on the heart. We can value too much what will pass away, but who we are in Christ is eternal. Erastus will not be introduced in heaven as the treasurer of a great city, but just like Quartus, as a brother.

Day 58

Thursday 14 May 2020

A poor widow

Then one poor widow came and threw in two mites.   (Mark 12:42)

In the summer of 1985 the Live Aid concert was held to raise funds for famine relief in Ethiopia. People around the world gave donations. In Ireland, an elderly widow went into a collection point, took off her wedding ring and dropped it into a donation box. When I heard that story I was challenged about sacrificial giving.

In Mark 12:38-40, Jesus condemns the scribes for their long robes, their overwhelming desire for recognition, and their long prayers. He also judges them for devouring widows' houses. In that society widowhood often meant extreme poverty and vulnerability. Its leaders had forgotten God was a Father to the fatherless and a Husband to the widow. Israel had become apostate and bereft of compassion.

But it was in such a place the poor widow, who Jesus saw, gave everything she had. Her poverty is so spiritually rich. It tells us first that Jesus watched. We marvel at the words Jesus said and the power of His miracles. But it is important to understand that Jesus sees what others, including ourselves, do not. He watched the people He came to save. And what He sees He assesses perfectly. That day He saw many rich people making a show of how much they could give. The Lord sees the pure heart. He also sees pride in our hearts. He watched the poor widow. He saw her poverty and her complete faith in God.

She did not hesitate or ponder what she was about to do. She didn't stop to see if others would notice and perhaps come to her aid. No, she threw in the two mites, not in despair but, I believe, cheerfully. It was an act of sacrifice knowing that God loves a cheerful giver, and that He would be a Husband to her. She threw in both the mites she had. These were *lepta*, the smallest coin in Judaea, worth around 2p today. She gave everything she had. I do not believe God did not respond to such faith.

When Hudson Taylor lived in Hull, where I was born, he spent a lot of his time sharing the Gospel and doing what he could to address poverty in the city. One day a man approached him in need. Hudson had a florin in his pocket (worth two shillings), but he needed it to pay for his lodgings. He wished at that moment that he had two separate shillings so that he could have given one to the man and kept one for his needs. He prayed to God and gave the man his florin. On returning to his lodgings there was a letter with a gift for his needs. That experience taught him to be totally dependent upon God. He took that experience to China and eventually formed the China Inland Mission. This organisation took the Gospel beyond the coasts of China into its heartlands. His was a step of faith we still see the fruits of to this day.

The Lord Jesus was born into poverty and lived His glorious life in poverty. At the cross, they took even His clothes. Last, of all, He gave Himself.

> "For you know the grace of our Lord Jesus Christ, that though He was rich, yet for your sakes He became poor, that you through His poverty might become rich" (2 Corinthians 8:9).

> Love so amazing, so divine,
> Demands my soul, my life, my all.

Day 59

Friday 15 May 2020

A secret disciple

Nicodemus, who at first came to Jesus by night, also came, bringing a mixture of myrrh and aloes, about a hundred pounds.

(John 19:39)

We all remember the story of Nicodemus. He was a Pharisee and a ruler of the Jews. He came to Jesus by night because he was afraid of his fellow Pharisees who rejected the Saviour. But the most important thing was that he did come to Jesus. He came respectfully and honestly. He recognised Jesus as someone who had come from God. He knew this was true because of the demonstration of the Lord's power. Nicodemus was searching, and expected a quiet spiritual conversation. But the Lord immediately confronts him with his need to be born again. Nicodemus, for all his learning and genuine spiritual desire did not understand. And the Lord goes on to reveal Himself as the Saviour in the glorious words of John 3:16, "For God so loved the world that He gave His only begotten Son, that whoever believes in Him should not perish but have everlasting life."

We next see Nicodemus in the Sanhedrin when the officers reported that they had failed to arrest Jesus. When they are asked why they were unable to complete their task, they replied, "No man ever spoke like this Man!" (John 7:46). How those words must have resonated in the heart of Nicodemus. He had heard the Saviour speak to him of new birth and the immensity of the love of God in Christ. When the group talked about the officers being deceived, he courageously tried to defend the Lord. His defence is dismissed by the sarcastic response, "Are you also from Galilee? Search and look, for no prophet has arisen out of Galilee" (John 7:50-52). Nicodemus was learning the real character of the company he kept.

John records the words of the Lord Jesus on the cross, "It is finished" (John 19:30). The Lord had spoken of being lifted up and how God's love would be displayed by the sacrifice of His only Son. It was not Peter, James or John who came forward to take the body of the Lord Jesus and to lay in the tomb. No, it was secret disciples who saw the sacrifice of the Lord of glory and sought permission to bury Him. This was not the act of fearful men, but of those who were beginning to understand that the love of God casts out fear. Nicodemus and Joseph of Arimathea were not lowly fishermen from Galilee. They were highly respected rulers at the centre of the government of Israel. But that day they ceased to be secret disciples, and no longer cared for their reputations; they only wanted to respond to the Saviour who had died on the cross.

Nicodemus and his friend Joseph teach us about the transforming love of Christ. It alone can change us from fearful and secret disciples into fearless and bold disciples who identify ourselves with the Son of God who loved us and gave Himself for us. And who, like Nicodemus, don't come empty-handed but ready to sacrifice. May that same redeeming love move us in our lives to worship, follow and serve the Saviour.

Day 60

Tentmakers

Paul departed from Athens and went to Corinth. And he found a certain Jew named Aquila, born in Pontus, who had recently come from Italy with his wife Priscilla (because Claudius had commanded all the Jews to depart from Rome); and he came to them. So, because he was of the same trade, he stayed with them and worked; for by occupation they were tentmakers. And he reasoned in the synagogue every Sabbath, and persuaded both Jews and Greeks. (Acts 18:1-4)

When I was very young, Friday evenings were the most exciting time for me. It was when my father sat in his chair, where we were never allowed to sit, and he would line up all his children and give each one of us our pocket money. The speed at which I got from my home to the corner shop to buy sweets would have challenged the world's greatest sprinters. I never once thought about what my pocket money cost. One day very, very early in the morning, my father took me to where he worked as a baker. I remember he sat me on a bench and I watched him mix the dough in big machines and slide loaves of bread into vast ovens. It was the day I learnt where the burns on his forearms came from, as he caught them on the oven sides, pushing the bread into the heat.

That experience taught me about my relationship with my Father in heaven. Even as mature Christians, we often think of God only as a provider. Of course, He is a provider. Every material and spiritual blessing comes from His gracious heart and hand. But, like Moses on Mount Nebo, He wants to take us up and show us the wonders of His work of grace. He wants us to enter into all that He has done and will do in Christ. He wants us to know Him.

We were made to work. Adam was a gardener, Jacob a shepherd, Ruth a farmworker and Esther a queen. There is a dignity about the work God gives us to do. We see this in Paul as he worked with his friends, Aquila and Priscilla, as a tentmaker in Corinth. There is a seamlessness between his manual work and his ministry in the synagogue. He told the Ephesians elders in Acts 20 he had not shunned to declare to them the whole counsel of God (verse 27). Then he added, "Yes, you yourselves know that these hands have provided for my necessities, and for those who were with me" (verse 34). The Lord Jesus worked as a carpenter – and from the cross, He ensures John cares for His mother, Mary.

So often we compartmentalize our lives. God sees them as a whole. It was as Adam worked in the garden of Eden that God came down. Enoch walked with God throughout the day. David learned communion with God as a shepherd. Ruth learned to trust God on a farm. Even today, in Christian service, we speak of tentmaking as a means to an end. God doesn't separate out our lives or treat our secular work as secondary. The Lord Jesus was never ashamed to be called the son of the carpenter or indeed the carpenter. It was as such that He manifested the majesty of the love and grace of God. And God seeks to witness to that same love and grace that He has poured into our hearts through the work He has given us to do.

> "And whatever you do in word or deed, do all in the name of the Lord Jesus, giving thanks to God the Father through Him" (Colossians 3:17).

Day 61

Sunday 17 May 2020

When angels sat down

And behold, there was a great earthquake; for an angel of the Lord descended from heaven, and came and rolled back the stone from the door, and sat on it. (Matthew 28:2)

And she saw two angels in white sitting, one at the head and the other at the feet, where the body of Jesus had lain. (John 20:12)

Angels are eternally active in the service of God. The Bible, at times in mysterious ways and at others in precise ways, gives us an insight into their service for God. This service is beautifully expressed in the life of the Lord Jesus. In Luke 1:19 the angel Gabriel introduces himself to Zechariah, "I am Gabriel, who stands in the presence of God." This mighty angel was sent to announce, in the temple of the Lord, the birth of John the Baptist. Later, it is not to the temple but to the lowly town of Nazareth that Gabriel was sent from the presence of God to announce the birth of Jesus (verse 26). An angel told a few shepherds of the birth of Jesus, and those shepherds saw and heard a heavenly host fill the night sky with praise to God that Christ, the Saviour, had been born.

After Jesus was tested in the wilderness, Matthew and Mark tell us angels came to minister to the Lord (Matthew 4:11). When the grace of God was demonstrated to Jacob, in Genesis 28, he saw a vision of angels ascending and descending on a ladder set up on earth. Jesus tells Nathaniel, "Most assuredly, I say to you, hereafter you shall see heaven open, and the angels of God ascending and descending upon the Son of Man" (John 1:51). God's grace was perfectly revealed in His Son. That grace opened heaven to see the activity of angels subject to the Person of Christ. This will be seen again on earth during the Lord's millennial reign, but its evidence was demonstrated in the earthly ministry of the Lord Jesus.

That ministry led to the Garden of Gethsemane. It is in that garden we behold the agony of the Saviour as He faced the cross and all that it meant to save us. In that solemn hour, the disciples fell asleep. But angels did not. And in all the tenderness of heaven, one comes to strengthen the Lord (Luke 22:43). A little later in Matthew 26, when Peter raises his sword to defend the Lord, the Lord says, "Do you think that I cannot now pray to My Father, and He will provide Me with more than twelve legions of angels?" (Matthew 26:53). But there was a place where angels could not go: they could not speak, and they could not act. Their activity was to watch in holy amazement as their Lord suffered and died.

For centuries the cherubim of solid pure gold had stood motionless, looking down on the blood sprinkled on the mercy seat, blood which could never take away sin. On the resurrection day, an angel rolled the stone away from Lord's tomb, not to let the Lord come out, but to show it was empty. And the angel sat down upon the great stone. When Mary looked into the Lord's tomb, "she saw two angels in white sitting, one at the head and the other at the feet, where the body of Jesus had lain" (John 20:12). Angels bear witness to the deity, manhood, ministry, suffering, resurrection, ascension and return of the Lord Jesus. And there was a day when angels ceased from their activity and sat down. They sat down to remind us of the Saviour's glorious, perfect and eternal work of salvation. And to remind us to worship the One they never cease to serve.

Day 62

Monday 18 May 2020

The burden of love

"So he went to him and bandaged his wounds, pouring on oil and wine; and he set him on his own animal, brought him to an inn, and took care of him. On the next day, when he departed, he took out two denarii, gave them to the innkeeper, and said to him, 'Take care of him'". (Luke 10:34-35)

There was once a high-ranking civil servant who often entertained important guests from other countries. On one occasion, the chief guest was a French diplomat. The civil servant also invited his father, who was a godly man, to the event. In the course of the evening, as guests mingled and talked, the civil servant noticed his father was in deep conversation with the French diplomat. He joined them and discovered that his father was talking to the eminent guest about his soul. Quickly the son found an excuse to lead the Frenchman away. Some weeks later, the father died. By the graveside, the son looked at the flowers and many cards which expressed how much different people valued his father's spiritual care. He came across a beautiful array of flowers with a small card which read, "To the man who cared for my soul." It was from the French diplomat.

In the New Testament, there are two ways care is expressed. One is anxious concern. The kind of care that Jesus identified in Martha's life: "Martha, Martha, you are worried and troubled about many things" (Luke 10:41). It was those cares that distracted her from the Saviour. And it was the same cares Peter asks us to cast upon the Lord Jesus: "casting all your care upon Him, for He cares for you" (1 Peter 5:7).

The other way care is expressed is as a watchful, genuine and responsive interest. We see this shepherd-like care in Peter's second letter, "Moreover I will be careful to ensure that you always have a reminder of these things after my decease" (2 Peter 1:15). Peter was as fully committed as a spiritual shepherd at the end of his life as when the Lord first called him to shepherd the flock of God. That was the kind of man the father in our story was. The Lord Jesus describes in the story of the Good Samaritan His own care for the lost in the words, "and took care of him" (Luke 10:34), and He speaks of the responsibility He gave to the innkeeper, "Take care of him" (Luke 10:35). In this beautiful story the Lord Jesus conveys His care for the lost and His continued care for us when we have been found.

The Lord wants His caring ministry to be evident in our lives. He wants us to care for the souls of our neighbours and for the people of God. Paul writes of his concern for all the churches in 2 Corinthians 11:28, and he writes of Timothy, "I have no one like-minded, who will sincerely care for your state" (Philippians 2:20). Interestingly, in these verses he uses care in the sense of a burden. It is the burden of love that the Lord carried, and it is the burden, by His grace, He wants us to carry.

Day 63

Tuesday 19 May 2020

The graph of love

"Yes, I have loved you with an everlasting love;
Therefore with lovingkindness I have drawn you."

(Jeremiah 31:3)

A wise brother once told me that it is when we are relatively young that we have so many demands placed on us. These demands include responsibilities towards each other, our children, our families, our Christian fellowship and our work. The pressures can be intense. All the time, we have to deal with small and large changes. On occasions, we can anticipate change, but at other times it comes unexpectedly. Today we are experiencing worldwide sudden change on a scale we never imagined.

For several years June and I organised a young Christian couples' weekend to encourage them in their marriages and family life. We often started the weekend by asking each couple to individually draw a graph representing their experiences throughout married life. Then we asked them to compare the results and talk together about the joys and challenges they had faced. One year, when a couple did this exercise, the wife's graph was, as you would expect, a history of the highs and lows of married life. The husband's chart was a straight line!! We had the sense of his not being fully committed to the process. But it struck me that he had, unintentionally and simply, described something we should never lose sight of – the eternal and never-changing love of God: "I have loved you with an everlasting love."

God is love. That was true before the world began. It is true now and will be true when this world ceases to exist. But on this tiny planet God has revealed the immensity of that love in the Lord Jesus Christ. How could we ever truly know God existed or that His nature was love? Only by His coming into the world which He made and we inhabit; by God becoming man and revealing the wonder of His love directly in the Person of the Lord Jesus Christ.

If you had put the two graphs of our young couples together to represent their journeys, you would still not have the full picture. There is a missing line, the constant love of God. It is the line expressed in the words of the prophet Jeremiah, "Therefore with lovingkindness I have drawn you."

God's eternal and constant love also traces the path of our lives. It was the love known by Jacob – "the God that shepherded me all my life long to this day" (Genesis 48:15, Darby Trans.); by David – "You are with me" (Psalm 23:4); by Paul – "The Lord stood by me" (2 Timothy 4:17, ESV); and expressed by the Lord Jesus – "I will never leave you, nor forsake you" (Hebrews 13:5).

When my daughter, Anna, was very young, we were travelling home late one night after a long weekend. She was looking through the rear window of the car, watching the moon in the clear night sky. Then she asked me, "Dad, why is the moon moving?" I replied, "The moon isn't moving, we are!" Sometimes we are close to the Lord, and sometimes we move away from Him, at times a long way. But He never moves away from us:

> "Yes, I have loved you with an everlasting love;
> Therefore with lovingkindness I have drawn you."
> (Jeremiah 31:3).

Let that love flood our hearts today.

Day 64

Wednesday 20 May 2020

The compassion of God

"And should I not pity Nineveh, that great city, in which are more than one hundred and twenty thousand persons who cannot discern between their right hand and their left—and much livestock?"
(Jonah 4:11)

There are many prophets in the Old Testament, but none more complex than Jonah. And through His disobedient servant God shows us His heart of compassion. God sends a great wind and prepares a great fish, to ensure His wayward servant would save a great city of more than 120,000 people. But Jonah had lost the sense of God's compassion in his own heart and tried to distance himself from a people who most needed his ministry. And God prepares a plant, and finally a tiny worm, to patiently teach Jonah about His heart of love.

I have found myself during lockdown thinking of the compassion of God. Like Jonah, we can become hardened towards a world that is so far from God. We can forget God's "longsuffering toward us, not willing that any should perish but that all should come to repentance" (2 Peter 3:9). God's desire to bring people to Himself by opening their hearts to the Lord Jesus has not diminished. God has chosen to convey His Gospel through the witness of His people. Jonah was chosen to be a witness for God. And despite all that he knew about the character of God, he decided to attempt to run away from God's presence and his own calling. We cannot run away from God.

God intervenes in Jonah's life in the most powerful way by sending a great wind and causing a storm which endangered the ship and everyone in it. Yet Jonah in all his distance from

God was able to sleep soundly through the storm. He had to be woken up to understand the situation and explain what he had done. Jonah was prepared to sacrifice his life for the strangers travelling with him. He showed compassion! It is then that God prepares a great fish and Jonah spends three days and three nights in the deep. It is astonishing that God uses His most disobedient prophet to illustrate the obedience and love of Christ and where that love took Him before He emerged from death in all the power and glory of His resurrection.

So Jonah was called again to go to Nineveh and preach. There was not a people further away from God nor a message so simple. The whole city turned to God in repentance, and God responded with compassion. But Jonah did not rejoice with heaven. Instead, he was angry that God had been so gracious to Nineveh. God acts with the same grace towards His bitter servant. He prepares, not a great wind or great fish but a simple plant, and then amazingly a tiny worm which destroyed the plant. He does this is to reveal in Jonah a pity for something so transient. Then He powerfully asks, "Should I not pity?" Should God not show compassion?

The Lord Jesus uses Jonah, despite all his failings, to illustrate His own death and resurrection and to convict the hearts of the scribes and Pharisees in Matthew 12:38-41. Jonah is also a warning to us not to lose contact with the heart of God. Jonah described God as "a gracious and merciful God, slow to anger and abundant in lovingkindness" (Jonah 4:2). But Jonah did not feel that grace, mercy and lovingkindness in his own heart toward those who needed it so much.

May God protect us from losing compassion towards those who so desperately need the grace of God that has saved us, and that keeps us. And may He grant us the power and courage to witness to the God of all grace with tender hearts and to join heaven in rejoicing over everyone who comes to the Saviour.

Day 65

Thursday 21 May 2020

Not a hoof shall be left behind

Then Pharaoh called to Moses and said, "Go, serve the Lord; only let your flocks and your herds be kept back. Let your little ones also go with you." But Moses said, "You must also give us sacrifices and burnt offerings, that we may sacrifice to the Lord our God. Our livestock also shall go with us; not a hoof shall be left behind." (Exodus 10:24-26)

In his last meeting with Pharaoh, Moses said "not a hoof shall be left behind." Moses was describing God's complete redemption. The children of Israel left nothing in Egypt. Their flocks identified them. They were and had always been shepherds. Jacob, their father, took 20 years to rear his flocks while also caring for and bearing the cost of shepherding the flocks of Laban, his uncle (Genesis 31). Jacob knew the value of what God had given him. We see the skill of Jacob in the wisdom of Joseph when he managed the grain stores of Egypt to save a nation. Joseph knew what was valuable and how to use it to the glory of God. Moses valued everything that belonged to his people because it was what God had given them. And they needed their flocks to serve God in sacrifice and worship (verse 26). It was from those flocks that the Passover lambs were taken. Moses ensured nothing was left behind when he led his people out of Egypt. Interestingly in Jonah 4:11 God placed great value on livestock. He saved the people of Nineveh – and what they possessed – so that they could use these resources in devotion to God.

The challenging question these verses pose to me is, "How much do I leave in this world?" Paul writes to the church at

Corinth, "You were bought at a price; therefore glorify God in your body and in your spirit, which are God's" (1 Corinthians 6:20). To the church at Rome he writes, "I beseech you therefore, brethren, by the mercies of God, that you present your bodies a living sacrifice, holy, acceptable to God, which is your reasonable (spiritually intelligent) service" (Romans 12:1).

We have one life to live for the Saviour: body, soul and spirit. We don't, like the Israelites of old, present a valuable but dead sacrifice, rather a living sacrifice. God has redeemed us completely and given us life abundant. Our living sacrifice is to be seen in our worship, fellowship, relationships, homes and work and through the use of our money, resources and time. It is expressed in all the joys, challenges and sorrows of life. Our living sacrifice is characterised by love, joy, peace, longsuffering, kindness, goodness, faithfulness, gentleness and self-control. This happens through the transforming power of God and the inward change it makes in our lives.

We express this sacrificial life in a world to which we do not belong, but in which we are to be a blessing. This world will continually seek to conform us to its likeness. Moses would not leave a hoof behind. I need to value and use what God has given me in the light of my complete redemption and for His glory. The strength to do this comes from the Saviour, who said, "I have overcome the world" (John 16:33) and by our faith which is the victory that has overcome the world (1 John 5:4-5).

Day 66

Friday 22 May 2020

A key we should always carry

Let the word of Christ dwell in you richly in all wisdom, teaching and admonishing one another in psalms and hymns and spiritual songs, singing with grace in your hearts to the Lord. And whatever you do in word or deed, do all in the name of the Lord Jesus, giving thanks to God the Father through Him. (Colossians 3:16-17)

There is an interesting progression in Colossians 3:16-17 and it begins with the word "Let". This tiny word expresses the willingness that is needed for the word of Christ to dwell in our hearts richly. The experience of the two disciples on the road to Emmaus is a good example of what Paul is explaining. The Lord Jesus drew near to walk with them and talk to them of things concerning Himself. After He disappeared, they said to each other, "Did not our heart burn within us while He talked with us on the road, and while He opened the Scriptures to us?" (Luke 24:32). Christ dwelt in their hearts as He unfolded the wisdom of God in His pathway of suffering that led to glory. First, the Lord had to admonish them because of their lack of understanding, and their hesitant faith, which He called slowness of heart. Admonition is intended, not only to identify problems, but to clear them away and replace them with the blessing of spiritual teaching. The Lord in grace emptied their hearts of spiritual poverty to fill them with Himself. It was this ministry which caused them to compel Him to stay with them and gave them the joy of seeing the resurrected Saviour. We should never, ever forget that Christ should always be the centre of our ministry in all its forms.

There are two responses to the word of Christ dwelling in us richly. The first is worship in song. The Psalms express the wide scope of praise and worship. Hymns emphasise the single object of praise – God. Spiritual songs celebrate the spiritual blessings we have in Christ. During the lockdown, June and I have not been entirely alone. Early every morning, in the evening (and often in between), and as I write, we have a visitor. He is very conscious of social distancing, so, instead of coming into our home, he always sits on the highest branch of the large tree at the end of our garden. He is a blackbird. And every day he sings his heart out. Isn't it amazing that one of the smallest of God's creatures has such a joyous sound? Grace, in our hearts, puts joyous songs on our lips: the sacrifice of praise. This is expressed when we meet together and join our voices as one in harmony to God. We are often aware of our limited musical ability, and we shouldn't be careless in our singing. But perhaps we don't realise the pleasure that God has listening to the melody of our hearts addressed to Him, as we contemplate the wonder of His grace. This melody is sanctified by the ministry of the Holy Spirit of God and the Son of God. We should also raise our hearts to God in praise during the day when we are touched by that same grace. You sense this when Paul's heart was filled with the wonder of the Lord standing by him and he writes a song that was, I believe, in his heart at that moment, "To Him be glory for ever and ever. Amen" (2 Timothy 4:18).

The second response is work. The word of Christ richly dwelling in our hearts equips us for all the practicalities of life, both at its most menial level and also at its highest level. Truly heavenly-minded people are the most practical of people. Worshippers are workers. Those who offer "the sacrifice of praise to God" are also those who "do not forget to do good and to share, for, with such sacrifices, God is well pleased" (Hebrews 13:15-16). "Let" is the key of obedience which allows the unbounded richness of the grace of our Lord Jesus to flood into our lives. It is a key we should always carry.

Day 67

Fellowship

And they continued stedfastly in the apostles' doctrine and fellow-ship, and in breaking of bread, and in prayers.   *(Acts 2:42, AV)*

Last year for the first time many of us were at Ednam for the Borders Conference. It was an encouraging and happy weekend of fellowship and ministry. We expected to be there again this weekend, but the present crisis has prevented this from happening. The past weeks have taught us about the importance of our fellowship in Christ. Adam's first experience of fellowship was with God, and it defined all his other relationships. Satan destroyed that relationship. Since then, we have a history of attempting to fill the purpose for which we were created – fellowship with God – with a multitude of idols. But down the same ages, through the line of faith, from Abel onwards, there has been fellowship with God.

God made Himself known to Enoch and Noah. They walked with God and found grace in His sight. God manifested Himself to Abraham, Isaac and Jacob, and they built altars to worship the God who blessed them. It was God who initiated this remarkable fellowship between man and his Creator. God formed a nation, redeemed that nation of Israel and led them by one man, Moses, into the wilderness. It was there God expressed to Moses His desire to dwell amongst people. Later, through David and Solomon, a temple was built and, as with the Tabernacle, God filled it with His glory as He came down to dwell with His people. That glory was removed because of the nation's disobedience and persistent idolatry. Ezekiel describes how slowly the glory departed, which illustrated the sadness of the heart of God. It was the same sadness the Lord Jesus expressed when, as Immanuel, He dwelt here: "How often I wanted to gather your children together, as a hen gathers her brood under her wings, but you were not willing!" (Luke 13:34). The Lord's experience of rejection intensified as He also endured the bitter pathway from Gethsemane to Calvary. It is fully expressed in those awful words from the cross, "My God, My God why have You forsaken Me?" (Matthew 27:46).

The Lord Jesus through the sacrifice of Himself and His resurrection has brought us into fellowship with His Father. The Holy Spirit indwells us. Like the gold-covered boards of the tabernacle which were invisibly linked by the rod that ran through them, we are one in Christ Jesus. The present crisis may restrict how we gather but cannot destroy what God has established. We have reminded ourselves since the beginning of lockdown that nothing can "separate us from the love of God, which is in Christ Jesus our Lord" (Romans 8:39). But lockdown has made us realise how much we value the fellowship of the people of God. It has challenged me to do all that I can to support my fellow Christians and not cause difficulty.

"A brother is born for adversity" (Proverbs 17:17). When trouble comes, we should see it as an opportunity to demonstrate the love of God. And not to allow things to divide us. God wants to enrich not impoverish us. Thank God, there is a friend who sticks closer than a brother (Proverbs 18:24). We have a Saviour who does not separate Himself from us. He cares for us individually and He cares for the Church He loves. He will never leave us or forsake us. Lockdown has brought isolation. Sin isolated us from God, but the sacrifice of Christ has brought us into the arms of God the Father and into a fellowship of divine love. I think the Lord is using lockdown, to bring us into closer fellowship with Himself, to teach us humility, and transform us by His overwhelming grace. As we emerge from lockdown, let us do all that we can to value, protect and build up one another in love and enrich our fellowship and its testimony to our Saviour.

Day 68

Sunday 24 May 2020

The Lord's Supper

For as often as you eat this bread and drink this cup, you proclaim the Lord's death till He comes.　　　　　　*(1 Corinthians 11:26)*

It never ceases to amaze me to think of the Lord Jesus Christ in glory delighting in His people remembering Him. I first started going to the Lord's Supper as a young Christian, and it was some time before I contributed. However, I did feel what Peter expressed on the Mount of Transfiguration when he told the Lord it was good to be there. The Lord Jesus only asked us to do two things which are expressed physically. One is baptism, which we usually only do once. The other is to remember Him by breaking bread and drinking wine, which we usually do at the beginning of the week. I had been taught earlier in my Christian life that I needed to be baptised, and that the Lord Jesus wanted me to remember Him. Christendom has added centuries of complexity to the holy simplicity of what the Lord asks us to do. A dear brother who taught us so much from the Bible said that in the Scriptures what is most profound is expressed with the greatest simplicity.

It is good to reflect on why the Lord Jesus over 2000 years ago occupied an upper room to institute the simplest supper after the celebration of the Passover. The Passover looked forward to the day when God would, as Abraham explained to Isaac, provide a lamb (Genesis 22:8). John the Baptist announced the fulfilment of the prophetic aspect of those words when he saw Jesus, the true paschal lamb, and said, "Behold the Lamb of God who takes away the sin of the world" (John 1:29). It was the Lord Jesus Himself who expressed His feelings towards His disciples when He said, "With desire I have desired to eat this Passover with you" (Luke 22:15). John writes, "Now before the Feast of the Passover, when Jesus knew that His hour was come that He should depart out of this world unto the Father, having loved His own which were in the world, He loved them unto the end" (John 13:1). What did the Lord Jesus want us to understand and never cease to remember? He wanted us to remember Him, and to understand the depth of His love for us and the price He paid for our redemption. The Lord conveys what was in His heart in two words, "Remember Me". And in two everyday and simple foods, bread and wine, He conveys the power, beauty and sacrifice of His peerless life. In doing so, He invites us into His presence as those who He brought to Himself one by one – each with our own appreciation of "the Son of God, Who loved me, and gave Himself for me" (Galatians 2:20). He also draws us together as part of the Church of Christ, so that with one heart we can worship Christ who "loved the church, and gave Himself for her" (Ephesians 5:25).

It is a joy to simply remember the Lord. We look back to Calvary and trace the wonder of the God of love. We look up and worship our glorious Saviour in heaven. And we do this looking forward to His promised return to bring us into the Father's house. When Mary poured her expensive oil in worship upon the Lord, its fragrance filled the house and also rested on those present.

I think it was a conscious decision of the early disciples to remember the Lord Jesus on the first day of the week. We begin the week in the Lord's presence and in the atmosphere of His divine love. In doing so, we are empowered to live in its reality.

Day 69

Monday 25 May 2020

The Vinedresser

But the fruit of the Spirit is love, joy, peace, longsuffering, kindness, goodness, faithfulness, gentleness, self-control. (Galatians 5:22-23)

If you visit the Geneva region of Switzerland in the summertime, you will see the lower slopes of the mountains covered in grapevines, packed with grapes. It is a pleasure to be there when the first harvest of grapes is brought into the local caves. You can buy bunches of beautiful sweet grapes and also watch them being pressed before they are stored for winemaking. It is a joy to stand by the press with glass in hand to drink the juice as it flows out. There is no better taste of summer in the Alps!

In Galatians 5:22-23 Paul uses the metaphor of fruit to describe the life of the Lord Jesus Christ reproduced by the Holy Spirit in our lives as a result of walking in fellowship with the Lord Jesus. Paul tightly packs these extraordinary characteristics of the fruit of the Spirit into two verses of Scripture, like a bunch of grapes. The Lord Jesus uses grapes as an illustration of the fruit of the Spirit when, in John 15, He says:

"I am the true vine, and My Father is the vinedresser. Every branch in Me that does not bear fruit He takes away; and every branch that bears fruit He prunes, that it may bear more fruit. You are already clean because of the word which I have spoken to you. Abide in Me, and I in you. As the branch cannot bear fruit of itself, unless it abides in the vine, neither can you, unless you abide in Me. I am the vine, you are the branches. He who abides in Me, and I in him, bears much fruit; for without Me you can do nothing" (John 15:1-5).

D.L. Moody commented as follows on the Fruit of the Spirit:

> "Love is the first thing ... Someone has said that all
> the other eight can be put in terms of love. Joy is love
> exulting; peace is love in repose; long-suffering is love
> on trial; gentleness is love in society; goodness is love
> in action; faith is love on the battlefield; meekness is
> love at school; and temperance is love in training."*

But if you visited Switzerland in the wintertime, you would see the same slopes covered with individual grapevines that have neither leaves nor fruit. They look barren and lifeless. Sometimes we can be tempted to feel like those branches look: failing and fruitless. But there is a person who never thinks about these plants in this way – the vinedresser, who works skilfully, patiently and tirelessly on each branch, preparing them to be fruitful. He knows they have life in the vine. And he knows they are capable, in the words of the Lord Jesus, of producing fruit, more fruit and finally much fruit (John 15:1-5).

The vinedressers on the Jura slopes of Switzerland care deeply for their vines. But they are not connected to their plants as we are to our vinedresser. Our Vinedresser is not a paid expert. He is our Father; the God and Father of our Lord Jesus Christ. We often consider the grace of the Lord Jesus in stooping from glory into this world to become our Saviour. We often think of the Holy Spirit stooping down from heaven to be in us and with us. But how often do we think of the Father stooping down? He does this with all the gentleness and wisdom of His heart of love to make us like Jesus, His glorious Son. Never allow Satan to diminish the value God has placed on you. We cost the blood of His own Son. The Father cherishes our lives, and despite all our shortcomings, failure and wilfulness, He never ceases to act in all the patience of His marvellous grace and loving heart towards us, to make us fruitful until the day He brings us home.

* *Day by Day with D L Moody*, selected by Emma Moody Fitt (granddaughter); Chicago: Moody Press 1977

Day 70

The fruit of the Spirit: Love

But the fruit of the Spirit is love … (Galatians 5:22)

God is love. So it is no surprise that the first attribute of the fruit of the Spirit is love. The Lord Jesus Christ perfectly expressed the love of God, and the Holy Spirit produces this love in the lives of Christians. In Romans 5:5 Paul explains that the love of God has been shed abroad in our hearts. It enables us to respond in love to the One who has loved us, and it enables us to love others as God loves. The Lord Jesus describes this love in John 13:34-35. It was a new commandment He gave them to love one another in the same way He had loved them. By this love people would know we are the disciples of the Lord. He also speaks of the action of this love at the other extreme in Matthew 5:44: "But I say to you, love your enemies, bless those who curse you, do good to those who hate you, and pray for those who spitefully use you and persecute you."

This love is described in 1 Corinthians 13:4-8 as a love that never fails. This beautiful and powerful passage of Scripture is very challenging. We can, at times, struggle to express love even to our brothers and sisters in Christ. We feel guilty about this and try harder to do better. We try to force ourselves to love. But do you remember when you first discovered the love of God? When God saved you, His love flooded into your heart. Do you remember how natural it was to respond in love to God, to your new family and to your neighbours? Remember how Zacchaeus was willing to cheerfully give half of his wealth to the poor (Luke 19:8)? When the Lord opened Lydia's heart, she invites Paul and his co-workers into her house to stay (Acts 16:15).

And, in one of the most powerful examples of the transforming grace of God, the once-cruel jailer took Paul and Silas into his home, washed their wounds, and provided food. Joy filled his heart as he and his family were baptized (Acts 16:33-34).

The power to love comes from the One who loves us. The vine produces the branches, and the vinedresser cares for every branch. The branches simply abide. The power of life in the vine is manifested in the production of the fruit. It takes a long time to learn this vital lesson. And we have to relearn it, too, when we get drawn away from the Lord. But the Father's patient love which we first learnt, as the prodigal son did, when we were embraced in His arms, is a love which will not let us go and would always keep us near. I am no vinedresser, but it appeals to me that when vine branches are pruned, they are made shorter and consequently closer to the vine. It is from this place they draw more effectively from the life of the vine, to grow and become fruitful. God often uses events in our lives to humble us and bring us closer to the Saviour. This is always for our ultimate blessing. And the revelation of His divine love, through the power of the Holy Spirit in our lives, is always to His glory.

Day 71

The fruit of the Spirit: Joy

But the fruit of the Spirit is love, joy …   *(Galatians 5:22)*

There was once a Christian who could not contain his joy in the Lord. He would continuously add his loud "Amen" and "Praise the Lord" to the prayers and ministry he enjoyed so much. The church he attended became a little uneasy about his enthusiasm, but unsure about what to do. Until one of the elders came up with a great idea. The brother was quite poor and had a large family, so the elder suggested that, as winter was approaching, they bought the family some blankets. When they presented the brother with the blankets, he was overcome by their kindness. The elders then asked the brother if he would tone down his expressions of praise in the meetings. He said he would try. The first week he did very well. The second week he was struggling. The third week he stood and in his loudest voice said, "Blankets or no blankets, Praise the Lord!"

I can still remember a brother who did a similar thing in the meeting I grew up in. I don't think he was drawing attention to himself; he was simply expressing what we all feel in our hearts. This joy comes from the experience of God's love for us. We see it in the lame man in Acts 3:8 when he stood up, walked and leapt while praising God. And, at the other extreme of circumstances, we see it in Peter and John and later Paul and Silas, when they all experienced profound joy in the most adverse of circumstances (see Acts 5:41 and Acts 16:25). Of course, joy is not always loudly expressed, but it is something God wants us to enjoy as a reality in our lives. It is not reserved just for the special times like birthdays, anniversaries and weddings. God wants to pervade our lives with His joy – the joy we have when we look back to Calvary, look up into heaven to see Jesus living for us, and when we look on to the joy of His return. This joy is known by faith in the Lord Jesus: "Though now you do not see Him, yet believing, you rejoice with joy inexpressible and full of glory" (1 Peter 1:8). In Luke 15 the Lord Jesus illustrates the joy of the Trinity in finding the lost sheep, the lost coin and the lost son. This joy is our strength (Nehemiah 8:10). Its source is in God, not in ourselves. It is compelling that in the chapter where Jesus teaches us about how we live fruitful lives for God, He also says, "These things I have spoken to you, that My joy may remain in you, and that your joy may be full" (John 15:11). The joy is in the Person of Christ and becomes our experience through abiding in Him. John, who was there when Jesus said these words, later wrote, "that you also may have fellowship with us; and truly our fellowship is with the Father and with His Son Jesus Christ. And these things we write to you that your joy may be full" (1 John 1:3-4).

But there will be times in our lives which are very painful and bitter – times, like the present crisis, when faith will be tested, and we will feel at our lowest. It is not by mistake that God allowed the prophet Habakkuk to give voice to these experiences. He writes of a time when the fig tree may not blossom, the vines have no grapes, there are no olives, the fields produce no harvest, and there are no herds or flocks. Then, in the face of all this desolation, he writes, "Yet I will rejoice in the Lord, I will joy in the God of my salvation" (Habakkuk 3:18).

God has saved us; God will keep us and one day He will rejoice over us with singing. May we know His joy in our hearts, "blankets or no blankets."

Day 72

Thursday 28 May 2020

The fruit of the Spirit: Peace

But the fruit of the Spirit is love, joy, peace ...   *(Galatians 5:22)*

Peace is an elusive thing. The world speaks a lot about global peace and peace treaties between nations. But we have world leaders who use words which are anything but peaceful. Peace is missing in many communities, families and the hearts of individuals. Abuse of all kinds, and the sinfulness which mars this world, robs us of peace. Religion generally, and Christendom specifically, has caused terrible wars and waves of persecution. The world, despite all its progress in so many fields, seems as far as ever from enjoying lasting peace.

It was in such a world that the Saviour lived and, on the eve of His suffering its hatred and violence, He says to His disciples, "Peace I leave with you, My peace I give to you; not as the world gives do I give to you. Let not your heart be troubled, neither let it be afraid" (John 14:27). Only the Prince of peace could speak such words as He went into death to enable us to have peace with God (Romans 5:1). On the cross He turned to the thief to promise He would take him to Paradise (Luke 23:43). The word Paradise is Persian in origin. It referred to the Persian aristocrats' beautiful walled gardens, which were places of safety, tranquillity and delight. But the Lord was not merely promising Paradise. He promised the redeemed thief he would be with his Lord in Paradise. The peace is not primarily the place, but the Person.

As with all the attributes of the fruit of the Spirit, peace has its source in the Saviour. Paul, in Romans, writes about how we find peace with God through our Lord Jesus Christ. Then he writes in Philippians about how we daily experience the peace of God. "Be anxious for nothing, but in everything by prayer and supplication, with thanksgiving, let your requests be made known to God; and the peace of God, which surpasses all understanding, will guard your hearts and minds through Christ Jesus" (Philippians 4:6-7).

The apostles were not just writing beautiful words, but conveying what they had learned from the Prince of peace. They knew God's peace in the storms of life. They enjoyed the quietness and contentment that comes from living close to the Lord in all the circumstances of life. That was not always the case. In the Gospels, the disciples feared their boat would sink, and learned that Jesus was able to still the wind and the sea (Mark 4:35-41). On another occasion, Jesus walked on water as the disciples struggled to bring their ship to land. Peter also walked on water, before fear overcame him and he cried out for the Lord to save him. Immediately Jesus stretched out His hand and caught Peter and challenged his little faith. When they got into the boat, the wind ceased (Matthew 14:22-33). As a group of disciples, and as a single disciple, they cried to the Lord and the result was peace. What the Lord taught Peter when his faith was small became a reality when he experienced the Lord's presence and His peace, before the Sanhedrin, in Herod's prison and ultimately in his own martyrdom.

But Paul doesn't only teach us about the peace that passes all understanding. He gives us a pattern of a life of fellowship with Christ through which we learn that the God of peace is with us (Philippians 4:9). One day this world will be ruled by the Prince of peace. In the meantime we are invited to let the peace of God rule in our hearts (Colossians 3:15).

Day 73

Friday 29 May 2020

The fruit of the Spirit: Longsuffering

But the fruit of the Spirit is love, joy, peace, longsuffering…

(Galatians 5:22)

The first three attributes of the fruit of the Spirit are love, joy and peace. They have been described as Godward. The next three, longsuffering, kindness and goodness, are demonstrated towards others. There are two key words used for patience in the New Testament, the one expressing patience under trial, the other usually referring to tolerance towards difficult people. The one used by Paul in describing the fruit of the Spirit is more often used to emphasise patience towards other people. It is the thought of longsuffering. Without the experience of God's love, joy and peace in our hearts, showing longsuffering towards others is always going to be a tall order. But if we live in fellowship with God, daily seeking His presence, understanding and doing His will, then He will equip us to express patience towards everyone.

A brother once spent a lot of time writing a letter to another brother in Christ, whom he found particularly challenging. He felt it necessary to tell him a few home truths. When he proudly presented the letter to his wife for her comments, she read it carefully and then said, "This is a very well written letter. Now tear it up and throw it on the fire!" He was wise enough to follow her sound advice. When people rub us up the wrong way, irritating and annoying us, we generally go through a process. First, we try to subdue our inner feelings. This raises our blood pressure. If the problem persists we openly express our irritation and annoyance. Finally, we lose our temper. Some of us move quickly through this sequence of events. Others miss out the first two steps completely! Our relationship with God is vital to our relationship with others. If we are happy in the presence of God, patience, consideration and interest in others will flow out and replace sterile attempts to control ill will. We will begin to act towards others as God has acted towards us.

Peter was a man who always spoke his mind. At the end of his life, he writes in vivid terms of the wickedness of the world. In the final chapter of his second letter, he writes about the Lord's return and how people over time would scoff and say, "Where is the promise of His coming?" Then he writes, "The Lord is not slack concerning His promise, as some count slackness, but is longsuffering toward us, not willing that any should perish but that all should come to repentance" (2 Peter 3:9). Notice those words, "longsuffering toward us". Peter's age did not diminish his recollections of the Lord Jesus; it sharpened them. He remembered so clearly seeing the Lord Jesus on the Mount of Transfiguration and hearing the Father's voice saying, "This is my beloved Son." And he remembered so very clearly the longsuffering of the Lord Jesus towards him and how it had transformed him from a brash, self-confident fisherman into the kindly shepherd to the flock of God he became.

The Father wants to see the same transformation of each of His children into the likeness of His beloved Son. That is why Peter's last words to us are, "But grow in the grace and knowledge of our Lord and Saviour Jesus Christ. To Him be the glory both now and for ever. Amen" (2 Peter 3:18). Through the ministry of the Holy Spirit, that grace makes us longsuffering just like our Saviour and our Father.

Day 74

Saturday 30 May 2020

The fruit of the Spirit: Kindness

But the fruit of the Spirit is love, joy, peace, longsuffering,
kindness …   *(Galatians 5:22)*

Today is my mum's ninetieth birthday.

She sent all of her seven children to Sunday School. The one
I used to go to with my sisters decided to close for the summer.
To this day, I do not know how my mum found the Brethren
assembly on the high street in the area where we lived. But
the very next week we were packed off to what was to become
my spiritual home. I think it was the week afterwards that
I found myself with my sisters in the home of Mr Norman
Packer and his lovely wife, Isobel, for tea. There was so much
cake we thought we'd gone to heaven! Though I did not know
it then, I was experiencing the kindness of God in the hearts
of His people. The kindness of Mr and Mrs Packer and their
fellow believers gently and gradually led me to the Saviour and
to know the wonder of the kindness of God. I owe my mum a
great debt.

Paul writes about the kindness of God in his letter to Titus:
"For we ourselves were also once foolish, disobedient, deceived,
serving various lusts and pleasures, living in malice and envy,
hateful and hating one another. But when the kindness and the
love of God our Saviour toward man appeared, not by works of
righteousness which we have done, but according to His mercy,
He saved us, through the washing of regeneration and renewing
of the Holy Spirit" (Titus 3:3-5).

As recipients of God's kindness, we are encouraged to demonstrate it towards each other, "And be kind to one another, tenderhearted, forgiving one another, even as God in Christ forgave you" (Ephesians 4:32). Kindness witnesses to the fact that we are the children of God and the disciples of the Lord Jesus. In Matthew 11:30 the Lord says, "My yoke is easy, and My burden is light." The word "easy" could be translated "kindly": it is the same word as in Ephesians 4:32. We see the kindness of God in the Person of Christ.

Kindness expresses a compassionate and tender heart with a readiness to act sacrificially for the good of others. It is interesting that Luke records, in Acts 28:2, the kindness of the people of Malta following Paul's shipwreck, when he writes: "And the natives showed us unusual kindness; for they kindled a fire and made us all welcome, because of the rain that was falling and because of the cold." John's Gospel speaks of the Lord Jesus as the Son of God. It starts in eternity with the glory of His deity and His power as Creator. And it finishes on the shores of Galilee where the resurrected Saviour made a fire and cooked breakfast for His disciples, who had been toiling all night and caught nothing, until He guided their nets. John did not give us these details to expand the narrative, but to show us the kindness of God. In Matthew 10:42 the Lord recognises kindness in the giving of a cup of cold water. He values what we overlook.

I doubt I would be writing these words today were it not for the kindness of the Christian men and women I have mentioned. That kindness drew me to Christ. It is not in the vastness of the universe alone but also in the smallest detail of creation that the greatness and glory of God is manifested. We can talk eloquently about the love of God, but its reality is seen in the small, simple but powerful acts of kindness shown by those who know the heart of God.

Day 75

Sunday 31 May 2020

The fruit of the Spirit: Goodness

But the fruit of the Spirit is love, joy, peace, longsuffering,
kindness, goodness … (Galatians 5:22)

There was once a Christian who kept chickens on an extensive
piece of land behind his house. He noticed over a period of
time that his large brood of chickens seemed to be missing
one or two hens. He discovered that one of his neighbours was
relocating them! He told his wife he was going to go around
and confront the man. But his wife told him not to worry and
that she would sort it out. That afternoon she chose one of their
best chickens, plucked it and cooked a beautiful large chicken
pie. That evening she took it to their neighbour as a gift. The
couple never lost another chicken.

Goodness describes the moral quality of lives lived in fellowship
with God. Goodness is closely connected to kindness.
But commentators have suggested that kindness expresses
compassion and tenderness, whereas goodness sometimes acts
in a kindly way, as in our story, and sometimes in more forceful
ways. But it always has a moral challenge and conviction
associated with it. There are times when we need to be rebuked
and corrected. Proverbs teaches us that "a friend loves at all
times" (Proverbs 17:17). It also teaches us, "Faithful are the
wounds of a friend" (Proverbs 27:6). Goodness is not always
gentle, but it is always an expression of love. The Lord Jesus
describes His disciples as "the salt of the earth". Our lives should
have a moral edge to them. This shouldn't be self-righteousness
or give the impression we are better than others; it should be a
reflection of the Lord Jesus in our lives.

Barnabas is described as "a good man, full of the Holy Spirit and of faith" (Acts 11:24). We first meet Barnabas at the end of Acts 4 when he sold a field and brought all the proceeds to the Apostles (Acts 4:36-37). His action stands in contrast to the deception of Ananias and Sapphira in Acts 5:1-11. This marked Barnabas out as someone who, in response to the Saviour's love for him, became a self-sacrificing servant of Jesus Christ. It was Barnabas who saw the goodness of God in the life of Saul and brought him to the Apostles (Acts 9:27). How was the goodness of God shown to Saul? By the powerful presence of the Saviour in glory, His convicting words and by causing Saul to fall down blind. How did Paul describe the Person who did this to him? As "the Son of God who loved me" (Galatians 2:20). Following the remarkable work of God in Antioch, Barnabas was sent by the Apostles to encourage them. We are told he "encouraged them all that with purpose of heart they should continue with the Lord" (Acts 11:23). It was after this encouragement that we learn that the disciples of the Lord Jesus at Antioch were first called Christians. They didn't invent the name themselves; it was given to them by the society they lived in because their lives reflected Christ. The early disciples were recognised by their humility, grace and the "saltiness" of their lives which, in love, challenged the world they lived in.

Goodness is a vital part of the Christian testimony. The Lord Jesus went about doing good. After describing the richness of God's mercy, grace and kindness in Ephesians 2:4-9, Paul writes, "For we are His workmanship, created in Christ Jesus for good works, which God prepared beforehand that we should walk in them" (verse 10).

After remembering the Lord Jesus this morning, as we enter then into the responsibilities of a new week, may His goodness be seen in us.

Day 76

Monday 01 June 2020

The fruit of the Spirit: Faithfulness

But the fruit of the Spirit is love, joy, peace, longsuffering, kindness, goodness, faithfulness …   (Galatians 5:22)

Today we come to the final three attributes of the fruit of the Spirit in Galatians 5: faithfulness, gentleness, self-control. We can view love, joy, and peace as expressed towards God, and longsuffering, kindness, and goodness expressed towards others. All six attributes are shown in faithfulness, gentleness, and self-control. Faithfulness describes godly loyalty, trustworthiness, and reliability. It is a response in our lives to the faithfulness of God:

> "Through the Lord's mercies we are not consumed, Because His compassions fail not. They are new every morning; Great is Your faithfulness" (Lamentations 3:22-23).

In the Old Testament, we learn of God's faithfulness in creation, in the lives of the patriarchs and in the nation of Israel. Because of idolatry and departure from God, Israel became a divided kingdom and eventually suffered captivity in Assyria and Babylon. During the reigns of failing and wicked kings and then exile in strange lands, God remained faithful to His promises. We see the greatness of God's faithfulness most clearly as He brought His people out of captivity and back to the Promised Land He had given them. Against the dark background of exile, faithfulness to God by men like Daniel and women like Esther shone brightly. They did not rebel against God and take advantage of their new lives in Babylon. They chose to be faithful to God in distant lands that, as far we know, they never left. Daniel's faithfulness to God throughout the reign of Nebuchadnezzar until the days of Cyrus remained constant. And it was a source of great blessing to his people and the kings he served. His faithfulness did not change with circumstances. It stayed true, whatever the cost. The basis of this faithfulness was a complete and unshakeable trust in God and His promises.

The Lord Jesus perfectly expressed faithfulness to His Father. He is called "the faithful witness, the firstborn from the dead, and the ruler over the kings of the earth" in Revelation 1:5. This faithfulness is seen in His life, sufferings, death, and the glory of His resurrection.

Throughout the New Testament, Christians are encouraged to be faithful to the Lord Jesus in all the aspects of life – in their behaviour, relationships, marriages; as parents, employers and employees; in the smallest and most important details of their lives. And in their worship and service. Faithfulness is not an out-of-date or obsolete concept. It is a vibrant testimony to the character of God and the character of His children.

Interestingly, goodness and faithfulness appear next to each other in Galatians 5. In the parable of the talents, the lord, who is an illustration of the Lord Jesus, says to his faithful servants, "Well done, good and faithful servant; you have been faithful over a few things, I will make you ruler over many things. Enter into the joy of your lord" (Matthew 25:23). These words show how much the Lord Jesus values goodness and faithfulness, and links them to our future blessing. What value do we place on them?

Day 77

Tuesday 02 June 2020

The fruit of the Spirit: Gentleness

But the fruit of the Spirit is love, joy, peace, longsuffering, kindness, goodness, faithfulness, gentleness …　　(Galatians 5:22-23)

Christians should not be characterised by pride, arrogance, bullying or self-promotion. We are to be Christlike. In Matthew 11:29 the Lord Jesus describes Himself in these words: "I am gentle and lowly in heart." The word used for gentle in Matthew 11 is linked to that Paul uses for gentleness in Galatians 5. It is the thought of meekness. The fruit of the Spirit is seen in the behaviour of believers and it emerges from the work of the Holy Spirit in our hearts as we abide in Christ. Meekness is a spiritual attitude of dependence upon God. There is an absence of struggling and a calm trust in God's strength and blessing. We see this in Jacob when he wrestled with the Angel of the Lord. The angel dislocated Jacob's hip to end the experience. It is then that Jacob ceases to struggle and simply seeks the blessing of God. The rest of his life, though touched with great sorrow, was not a struggle for blessing but a ministry of blessing. We learn meekness from the Saviour. He teaches us not to try to escape limitations but, in the words of Peter, to "humble yourselves under the mighty hand of God, that He may exalt you in due time" (1 Peter 5:6).

I remember an occasion at work when I applied for a job in a department where I used to work and was well known. I was expected to return in a new role, but to everyone's surprise, I didn't get the post. I discovered that my Head of Department, who was not an easy man to work for, had blocked the move. I was furious and began to consider possible courses of action.

I remember praying about the issue, and the verse came to me, "who, when He was reviled, did not revile in return; when He suffered, He did not threaten, but committed Himself to Him who judges righteously" (1 Peter 2:23). I let the matter drop and felt a great sense of peace with what God had allowed. About a year later, I went on secondment to a department led by the Head of Department I would have worked for had my earlier application been successful. Within a short time, he promoted me to a senior role in his team. The experience taught me an important spiritual lesson. We can be misled into thinking that gentleness and meekness are signs of weaknesses. So we try to assert ourselves and fight for our rights or perhaps our pride. We don't pause and ask ourselves, "What is God teaching me?" The overriding answer is simple: to become Christlike. The Lord Jesus was "gentle and lowly of heart", but He was the most powerful man who ever lived in this world.

In the Old Testament Isaiah writes,

> For thus says the High and Lofty One
> Who inhabits eternity, whose name is Holy:
> "I dwell in the high and holy place,
> With him who has a contrite and humble spirit"
> (Isaiah 57:15).

And in the New Testament James writes, "Who is wise and understanding among you? Let him show by good conduct that his works are done in the meekness of wisdom" and then, "But the wisdom that is from above is first pure, then peaceable, gentle, willing to yield, full of mercy and good fruits, without partiality and without hypocrisy" (James 3:13, 17). These verses teach us that humility, meekness and gentleness are features of lives lived in communion with God; the lives of Christians who are "strong in the Lord and in the power of His might" (Ephesians 6:10).

Day 78

The fruit of the Spirit: Self-control

But the fruit of the Spirit is love, joy, peace, longsuffering, kindness, goodness, faithfulness, gentleness, self-control.

(Galatians 5:22-23)

The final attribute of the fruit of the Spirit mentioned in Galatians 5 is a very challenging one – self-control. Because it starts with "self" we can fall into the trap of thinking we do it. The "works of the flesh" are wilful actions of disobedience and self-interest. But the fruit of the Spirit is not an effort of the will. It is the cultivation of the life we have in Christ, the True Vine. The Spirit of God connects us to the Lord Jesus, and God the Father, the Holy Vinedresser, oversees our fruitfulness.

We tend to limit the idea of "control" to specific issues. For example, we think of temperance as controlling alcohol abuse. We tend to focus on those issues we have problems with, such as our pride, impatience and temper. God has given us many things to richly enjoy. And He has also clearly told us what we should not do. There are dangers in becoming absorbed and distracted by the good things God gives, such as possessions and careers. Demas was an example of a Christian who was in love with this present world. There is also the constant danger of giving way to sin in all its forms. David had a terrible fall caused by idleness and looking at a beautiful woman who was another man's wife. But self-control should not be isolated to single issues. It is a whole-life issue.

We have to grasp the depth and power of these words of the Lord Jesus: "I am the vine, you are the branches. He who abides in Me, and I in him, bears much fruit; for without Me you can do nothing" (John 15:5). The secret of producing the fruit of the Spirit, and in doing so avoiding spiritual dangers, is abiding in Christ. We need so much to respond to the Saviour's invitation to abide in Him. Obedience begins with abiding. Mary sat at the feet of the Lord Jesus to listen to His words. But in John 11 she learned to move when the Lord spoke to her. Astonishingly the Lord moved, with the incredible power of the One who is "the resurrection and the life," when He saw Mary's tears. When we move into the presence of God, He moves in our lives. He makes us Christlike. He directs our paths and empowers our service. Power for the Christian testimony does not come from our innovation, organisation and effort; it comes only from the presence of God. When we came to Christ, we understood, without any doubt, that we could never save ourselves. We needed the Lord Jesus to save us. The expression of the life we have in Christ is founded on the same principle – coming to Him and finding rest and all our resources in the Saviour. In this sanctuary the fruit of the Spirit is produced in us. This is the basis of God fulfilling His purposes through our lives to His glory.

We began our reflection on the fruit of the Spirit with some words D.L. Moody quoted:

> Love is the first thing ... Someone has said that all the other eight can be put in terms of love. Joy is love exulting; peace is love in repose; long-suffering is love on trial; gentleness is love in society; goodness is love in action; faith is love on the battlefield; meekness is love at school; and temperance is love in training.

Moody was a remarkable evangelist who was used of God to bring thousands of souls to Christ, and his ministry was influential in so many powerful ways. He understood that everything that is done for the glory of God begins in the presence of God. This is the presence we are invited into: "Abide in Me."

Day 79

Thursday 04 June 2020

Wise soul winning

He who wins souls is wise. *(Proverbs 11:30)*

I used to work with a very cheerful and outgoing colleague. He was always at the centre of every conversation and was a likeable man. But at the mention of God, he became outraged. If a disaster was in the news, he invariably blamed it on the God he didn't believe existed. Although we got on well together, he made it very clear he was not at all sympathetic to my faith. I worked with him for several years. One day we had lunch together, and for the very first time, he spoke with me about my faith in Christ. I remember the sense of excitement I had as the conversation developed. As we talked, another man, who was a Christian, sat with us. As he listened to our conversation, he joined in and in a very pointed way started speaking to my friend whom he had never met. Within moments my colleague left the table. I never got the same opportunity again to talk with a man who needed the Lord so much.

During the lockdown, I have thought a lot about personal evangelism. The earliest Christians blended their witness into their everyday lives. Of course, we know God worked powerfully at Pentecost and in Jerusalem, bringing thousands to faith in the Lord Jesus. But even this was based on a relationship with His people. This evangelism continued through the ministries of Philip, and the missionary journeys of Paul and Barnabas and men like Silas. But it is essential to look at the extraordinary backdrop to this evangelism. Centuries before, God had exiled His people, first in Assyria, then in Babylon, and scattered them further still. The extensive network of Jewish synagogues throughout Europe and the Near East emerged from those events. In the wisdom of God and through the judgement of His people, in grace He created places which became the starting points of Gospel outreach.

God always has a starting point in people's lives. This is, in the main, based upon relationships. He communicates through them even when they are damaged. The Lord Jesus connected with people in everyday situations. He understood them as individuals and reached out to them in their circumstances with the message of salvation. He did this in divine wisdom. Jesus was able to bring anyone to their knees by the glory of His presence. He did that with Paul. But He did not do this very often. He brought people to Himself by drawing near to them, understanding them and ministering to their needs.

If we are to lead others to Christ, we have to follow the Saviour's pattern. The grace of God always has a potent edge to it. The lives of Christians are meant to be challenging. Paul writes, "Walk in wisdom toward those who are outside, redeeming the time. Let your speech always be with grace, seasoned with salt, that you may know how you ought to answer each one" (Colossians 4:5-6). Paul speaks about the wisdom we need and the opportunities we should make and take to witness for the Saviour. Then he talks about our words being gracious, but at the same time always presenting the challenge and the blessing of the Gospel.

May God revive in our hearts the desire to win souls for Christ, to see the opportunities He presents, and give us the wisdom of the Saviour to share His love.

Day 80

Friday 05 June 2020

Grandma's spare room

Blessed are all those who put their trust in Him.　　　(Psalm 2:12)

When I was a young boy, I loved to go to my Grandma's to escape my many sisters. Grandma's spare room was my world where I could play, draw, and enjoy my own company. It was in that room I made two important discoveries. The first discovery was a dangerous one. One day I was feeling a little bored and looked for something interesting to do. The light switch caught my attention. In those days the whole of the front casing of a light switch could be easily unscrewed. Which is what I did, exposing the wires inside. I turned the switch on, but apart from the light coming on nothing else happened. Then for some reason which, to this day, I cannot explain, I decided to put my finger inside the light switch! When I got up off the floor, I had acquired a respect for electricity which I have never lost, and a very sore finger! I have used this story many times when I have preached the Gospel, to illustrate what it is to have faith in Christ, just like the diseased woman in Mark 5:28 who said to herself, "If only I may touch His clothes, I shall be made well." Through her hesitant touch she immediately discovered the power of the love of God in Jesus.

The Lord Jesus delights to respond to our faith in Him. Paul wrote to the young Church at Thessalonica, "We give thanks to God always for you all, making mention of you in our prayers, remembering without ceasing your work of faith, labour of love, and patience of hope in our Lord Jesus Christ in the sight of our God and Father" (1 Thessalonians 1:2-3). How quickly these young Christians were characterised by a living faith, love in action and a bright hope which lifted their hearts to God. God's power was demonstrated in their lives through faith.

The second discovery I made in my Grandma's spare room was two books inside an old cupboard. One was a big, old Bible, and the other a book called *"Seen and Heard"*. I asked my Grandma if I could have them. Those two books remained unread in my room at home for a long time. Then as a young teenager, I was challenged by the Gospel and began to read the Bible and also *"Seen and Heard"*. It was the story of the remarkable Scottish evangelist James McKendrick who was at the heart of the powerful revivals that took place on the East Coast of Scotland. The copy was signed by him. I was under conviction as I read its pages. But I wasn't sure I was saved until I came to page 116 where James McKendrick asked a woman why she didn't trust in Christ. She replied, "I do trust the Lord, but I am not saved". He quoted the verse, "Blessed are all those who put their trust in Him" (Psalm 2:12). He then said, "If the Lord has blessed all who trust in Him, what has He done with you?" The light shone into her heart as she realised she was saved too. As I read those words, the same light shone into my heart!

In my Grandma's spare room it was remarkable that God saved me from my own foolish actions. It was more remarkable that God ensured two books were left in an old cupboard and that He would direct a young boy to take them home and use them to open his heart to Christ. How much He is worthy of our complete and lifelong faith and worship!

Day 81

Saturday 06 June 2020

An old wooden chest

And you He made alive, who were dead in trespasses and sins, in which you once walked according to the course of this world.

(Ephesians 2:1-2)

In his letter to the Ephesians, Paul has three great themes – sitting, walking and standing. He uses these words as metaphors for our position in Christ in heaven, our daily lives as Christians and our witness in the world. In the first three chapters Paul writes about God's will, God's work and God's wisdom. Then in the last three chapters he writes about the believers walk, witness and warfare. The Spirit of God weaves these thoughts together, like the beautiful colours used in the Tabernacle.

I would like to reflect on the Christian's walk. Paul writes first about how we used to walk "according to the course of this world, according to the prince of the power of the air, the spirit who now works in the sons of disobedience" (Ephesians 2:2).

There was an eminent Chinese official whom the emperor valued immensely. But his fellow officials were jealous of the servant's status. And, as in the story of Daniel, they planned his downfall. The only thing they could find unusual about his behaviour was that every day he would go to a secret room in his house. They reported this to the emperor, suggesting the official was planning a coup. The emperor demanded to go to the room along with the members of his government. The faithful servant led the monarch and the people with him into an empty room. In the centre of the room was an old wooden chest. The emperor instructed the man to unlock and open the chest. Inside the chest were some ragged, dirty clothes. The emperor asked his official what the room, the chest and rags meant. The official told him that every day he came into the room and opened the chest, to remember that he was the son of poverty-stricken peasants and to be thankful that he now served his emperor.

Paul never lost the deep sense of how far away from God he had been. And as we know, he progressively describes himself as the least amongst of the apostles (1 Corinthians 15:9), then less than the least amongst all the people of God (Ephesians 3:8) and finally, the chief amongst sinners (1 Timothy 1:15). We like to compare these thoughts with his description of his meeting with the Lord Jesus when "a light shone around him from heaven" (Acts 9:3), "a great light from heaven shone around me" (Acts 22:6) and "a light from heaven, brighter than the sun, shining around me" (Acts 26:13).

Paul goes on to speak to the Ephesians about: walking in good works (Ephesians 2:10), walking worthy of the calling (4:1), walking in love (5:2), walking as children of light (5:8) and walking in wisdom (5:15). But he begins by reminding us from where "God who is rich in mercy, because of His great love with which He loved us" raised us up to make us "sit together in the heavenly places in Christ Jesus" (2:4-6). Such love bows our hearts in worship and empowers us to walk humbly with our God (see Micah 6:8).

Day 82

Sunday 07 June 2020

The House at Bethlehem

Behold, the star which they had seen in the East went before them, till it came and stood over where the young Child was. When they saw the star, they rejoiced with exceedingly great joy. And when they had come into the house, they saw the young Child with Mary His mother, and fell down and worshipped Him. And when they had opened their treasures, they presented gifts to Him: gold, frankincense, and myrrh. (Matthew 2:9-11)

The story of the wise men is rarely read when it is not Christmas. This is so engrained within our experience that we can be knocked off balance when we read the story at any other time. We have to beware of confining the word of God to particular times or circumstances. God's word is living and powerful and always has relevance.

The long journey of the wise men takes us first to Herod's palace. It was the corrupt centre of political and spiritual activity in Jerusalem. We learn powerful lessons about the wicked actions of tyrants, the sufferings of the innocent and rage against the Saviour. These things still happen today.

But then their journey takes them from the palace of a wicked king to a simple house in Bethlehem. The star, rather like the Holy Spirit, leads the wise men to the Person who came from the centre of heaven, not to the centre of a palace or even a temple but of that small house. It reminds us how God can bring seeking men from afar off to the Person of Christ. The wise men were comfortable and confident as they walked into Herod's palace. They were not overawed by his power. They were familiar with palaces and arrogant rulers. But what a difference when they were led by the star to Joseph's house in Bethlehem. They were filled with "exceedingly great joy" (Matthew 2:10) as they entered it. They were not surprised by the humble surroundings. There was no discussion about it being the right place. By faith, they walked into the house and saw the Son of God with His mother. They saw the manifestation of God's eternal love; God became small to demonstrate He was One heaven could not contain (1 Kings 8:27). Mary is mentioned, not to glorify her, but to reflect the wonder of the Lord Jesus' true humanity – born of a woman (Galatians 4:4). And the wise men fell down and worshipped Jesus.

They delighted to open their treasures: gifts of gold, frankincense and myrrh. When the shepherds of Israel went to see Jesus they had no gifts. They came just as they were, as we all come to the Saviour. The wise men came as worshippers ready to respond to the majesty of Christ. It was not the richness of their valuable gifts, but what those gifts represented that was so important. Gold decorated the Tabernacle and Solomon's temple, where God dwelt amongst His people. It reminds us of the Lord's deity and His dwelling in the world He had made. In John 12, Mary poured fragrant oil on the Lord Jesus. We are reminded by the frankincense of the Lord's life as a man. This life was lived in obedience to His Father and led to the cross. When the Lord died, there was no recognition by Israel of Him as the Son of God and the Son of Man who lived here for us. But in John 19, Nicodemus, in fellowship with Joseph of Arimathea, brought a mixture of myrrh and aloes to bury the Saviour. The myrrh reminds us of the death of the Son of God who gave Himself in love for us at Calvary. God ensured that at the beginning of the life of Jesus in this world, wise men would offer prophetic worship to announce the wonder of Immanuel.

This morning we come to the simplicity of the Lord's supper. Like the wise men, we should come with joy in our hearts to fall in worship at our Saviour's feet, and respond in grateful praise to the One who is God, and became man to become our glorious Saviour.

Day 83

Monday 08 June 2020

Walking on water

Jesus went to them, walking on the sea.   (read Matthew 14:22-33)

One of my abiding memories of Israel was a trip on the Sea of Galilee in a fishing boat. It was a glorious day, and the water was like glass. I don't think I have been on open water when it was so still and peaceful. It was an impression of what it must have been like when the Lord stilled the sea. There are times in our lives when the Lord stills our fears and calms our souls by His presence.

The Lord Jesus had sent the disciples into the boat while He dismissed the crowd. How does one person send home five thousand men, besides women and children? Our government has trouble in the present circumstances controlling crowds on beaches and small groups on our streets. But the Saviour quietly sends home the vast company He had just fed, then climbs up a mountain and prays. What was it like for the Creator of the universe to be in the world He had made? He could have gone anywhere instantaneously. But He climbed mountains to pray and walked through waves to be with His own.

When Jesus walked on the sea, there was not a terrifying storm. But the wind was against them, the boat was far from land and the disciples were being tossed about in a rough sea. The world we live in is changeable. We face the storms of life which are difficult to travel through, and some of which are very threatening. We also know calmer paths. Jesus was teaching His disciples about how He would always be with them in their circumstances.

They thought He was a ghost. People are afraid of the presence of God. In a world that has become so absorbed by what is material, people are uncomfortable when God reveals Himself to give them peace: "Be of good cheer! It is I; do not be afraid" (verse 27). Peter's response, like ours, often begins with an "if": "Lord, if it is You ..." (verse 28). But he did put himself in the hands of the Saviour who says, "Come" (verse 29). And Peter walked on water to go to Jesus. Then comes the most testing challenge to our faith – do we look to Jesus or look at the dangers or cares that surround us? Peter was, as we are often are, overwhelmed by the situation. He began to be afraid and sink into the sea. And Jesus immediately responds to his cry, "Lord, save me!" (verse 30), by lifting him up.

A brother once told me the story of when he first went to sea as a young fisherman. He woke up in the middle of a stormy night; the boat was being battered, and he felt terrified. He got up and went to the bridge where he could see the powerful waves on all sides of the vessel and feel the wind howling across its bows. Then he saw the skipper calmly manoeuvring the boat through the storm and joyfully singing hymns! He knew then he was safe. The Lord Jesus wants us to know we are safe.

Matthew 14 does not start with calmness, but after Jesus lifted Peter out of the sea, they walked back together through the storm to the boat and the wind ceased (verse 32). We all know those two watchwords of lockdown, "Stay safe." The Lord Jesus wants us to walk with Him, by His grace, through all the experiences of our lives, knowing He will never let us go, knowing we are safe and, like the disciples, with our hearts filled with worship: "Truly You are the Son of God" (verse 33).

Day 84

The interception

Be clothed with humility. *(1 Peter 5:5)*

When I was at school I always felt lessons got in the way of cricket in the summer and rugby in the winter. I loved rugby and played in the school teams. We had a lot of success in competitions. My greatest moment was when I was playing in one game and intercepted a pass and ran from the halfway line to score a try under the posts. I was so proud. And I knew that day the sports page of the local newspaper would report on my try. I eagerly awaited the newspaper. And sure enough they reported my try – but devastatingly they credited the try to my friend Keith Bolton who couldn't run to save his life!

When I think about that incident now I think of Peter's words, "Be clothed with humility." Peter, like me and many others, was not a man who was naturally humble. He was full of self-confidence and thought that being self-confident had a place in spiritual things – and we know where that mistake led him.

But in chapter 5 of his first letter we see the transformation in the life of this dear man of God. He does not teach us to be clothed in humility without gently revealing the humility which marked him as a saint of God: "The elders who are among you I exhort, I who am a fellow elder and a witness of the sufferings of Christ, and also a partaker of the glory that will be revealed" (verse 1). Peter does not speak of himself as an Apostle called personally by his resurrected Saviour to shepherd the flock of God. No, he speaks of himself in humility as a fellow elder in fellowship with other elders, in caring for the people of God. And he reminds them of our suffering and glorious Lord and

Saviour, who is the Chief Shepherd. Fellowship in caring for the flock of God is so important. Paul describes how precious God's people are to Him when he says to the Ephesian elders, "Shepherd the church of God which He purchased with His own blood" (Acts 20:28). They are to be precious to us, too.

Humility is central to shepherding the flock of God. Peter instructs the elders to shepherd the Lord's people who were local to them, and to do this willingly, selflessly, gently and by example (verses 2-3) – in other words to shepherd as the Lord did. It is an enormous privilege and responsibility to care for God's people. That care needs to be characterised by humility and to be done in a fellowship which recognises and encourages the service of others. The example of humility in the lives of elders, which Peter first addresses, encourages humility amongst younger people, and then all the people of God: "Likewise you younger people, submit yourselves to your elders. Yes, all of you be submissive to one another, and be clothed with humility" (verses 5). Humility is something which prospers the people of God. By humbling ourselves under the mighty hand of God we are in the place where God can display His power. Peter had held the mighty hand of God when Jesus lifted him out of the sea, in Matthew 14. Later, in John 21, Peter was not afraid to cast himself into the sea to be close to the Saviour who that day called him to be a shepherd.

May the Lord Jesus clothe us with humility, so that He can demonstrate the power of His love and grace in our lives.

Day 85

Walking in good works

For we are His workmanship, created in Christ Jesus for good works, which God prepared beforehand that we should walk in them. (Ephesians 2:10)

The first time Paul uses the word "walk" in his letter to the Ephesians, it describes their past lives. In contrast, His next mention of "walk" is linked to good works. They had been delivered from the power of darkness and conveyed into the kingdom of the Son of His love (Colossians 1:13). Genesis describes Enoch, Noah, Abraham and Isaac as men who "walked with God". Paul doesn't use the word "walk" to describe a physical act. He uses it as a metaphor for daily Christian living in fellowship with God. It is uplifting to see God's work in the glory of creation. We see this in the wonders of our universe and the astonishing diversity, complexity and beauty of planet earth. But Paul also writes of God's workmanship in His new creation in Christ and the good works which manifest it.

There is a lighthouse built on the Bell Rock in the North Sea, 11 miles east of the Firth of Tay. Each stone was shaped on land and transported out to sea and fitted together on the Bell Rock until the structure rose to its height of 116 ft. There the Bell Rock Lighthouse has stood shining its light for the safety of shipping for over 200 years. One day Christ will present His Church to Himself. It will be made up of every blood-bought saint. Paul writes that Christ loved the Church and gave Himself for her and one day she will be seen in all her perfection and glory (Ephesians 5:25-27). It is built upon Christ: "On this rock, I will build My Church" (Matthew 16:18). Until that day of presentation, as members of that same church, we are to shine for Christ both individually and together in fellowship. We shine by God's work of grace in us, "created in Christ Jesus for good works".

Because we are saved by grace, we are almost afraid of the idea of good works. However, these are not done to obtain salvation, but to show we have salvation. The world coined the expression "do-gooders" to belittle righteousness. But when Peter spoke in the house of Cornelius to a Gentile audience, he referred to Jesus in this way, "God anointed Jesus of Nazareth with the Holy Spirit and with power, who went about doing good and healing all who were oppressed by the devil, for God was with Him" (Acts 10:38). Peter involves the whole of the Trinity in the Lord Jesus' ministry of doing good and healing. As Christians, we need to understand afresh how God wants to move in our lives for good. God had this in mind beforehand. In the New Testament, there are so many examples of people Jesus saved who immediately testified to their salvation by good works. Zacchaeus said, "Half of my goods I give to the poor" (Luke 19:8). Jesus didn't tell him to do that, but salvation produced the good work. Spiritual good works are selfless acts. Sometimes they emerge spontaneously from our hearts to a need presented to us by God. Sometimes God exercises us to do something for the rest of our lives. They characterise our service and spring from a genuine desire to please the Lord by benefiting others. They are free-will offerings. And God delights in the ministry of the Lord Jesus being carried out by His children when they go about doing good.

Each day is a fresh opportunity to "Trust in the Lord, and do good" (Psalm 37:3).

Day 86

Thursday 11 June 2020

Walk worthy

I, therefore, the prisoner of the Lord, beseech you to walk worthy of the calling with which you were called, with all lowliness and gentleness, with longsuffering, bearing with one another in love, endeavouring to keep the unity of the Spirit in the bond of peace.

(Ephesians 4:1-3)

Paul never saw imprisonment as a restriction to his service for the Lord, but as part of that service. Paul was a prisoner of the Lord. He discovered in Philippi, with his friend Silas, that a prison cell, however dark, could become a place of prayer, praise and witness. At the beginning of His Galilean ministry in Luke 4, the Lord Jesus speaks of coming to heal the broken-hearted and to set captives free. It was not Paul and Silas who were broken-hearted and captive that night in the jail at Philippi in Acts 16; it was the Philippian jailer. As the love of God flooded into his heart, it was healed, and he was set free from sin. Paul knew what God could do in prison.

Paul's imprisonment became a ministry which went far beyond even his own extensive travels. But this did not mean he didn't suffer as a prisoner. At the end of his life, Paul writes to Timothy about suffering in chains like a criminal but adds that God's word cannot be chained (2 Timothy 2:9). His prison ministry was painful, but God uses it to teach us about the liberty we have in Christ. And as a prisoner of the Lord Jesus, Paul lived in the dignity of his heavenly calling; he walked worthy. And he appeals to us to do the same. We are taught by God to live before Him in a way which honours Him whatever our status in life. John F. Kennedy, former president of the United States of America, visited the NASA space station when the plan to put a man on the moon was being developed. In the washroom he met a cleaner and asked what the man did. The man replied, "I am helping to put a man on the moon!" That man saw his menial job in the context of a great endeavour. We have to see our lives in the context of the will and glory of God. As the people of God, we are not merely cleaners or scientists, we are God's cleaners and God's scientists.

W.E. Vine explains that the word Paul uses for "calling" is always used in the New Testament of a calling which has a heavenly origin, nature and destiny. It brings us into all the blessing of God's love and grace, and it imparts a spiritual dignity to our lives. As such we are the children of God and we are to be characterised by the features of the Son of God: lowliness, gentleness and longsuffering. We are to bear with one another in love. God's love is displayed by our love for one another. We are to love each other as Christ loves us (John 13:34-35). And we are to endeavour to keep the unity of the Spirit in the bond of peace because Jesus prayed to the Father that His disciples would be one, "as You, Father, are in Me, and I in You; that they also may be one in Us, that the world may believe that You sent Me" (John 17:21).

By the power of the Holy Spirit and by expressing the unity and peace of the fellowship of life He has brought us into, we walk worthy to demonstrate Christ's love toward one another. In doing so, we glorify our Saviour and our Father in the world.

Day 87

Friday 12 June 2020

Walk in love

Therefore be imitators of God as dear children. And walk in love, as Christ also has loved us and given Himself for us, an offering and a sacrifice to God for a sweet-smelling aroma. (Ephesians 5:1-2)

Paul closes Ephesians chapter 4 with the words, "And be kind to one another, tenderhearted, forgiving one another, even as God in Christ forgave you" (Ephesians 4:32). Then chapter 5 begins by encouraging us to continually imitate God as children. What characterises the children of God? Kindness, tender-heartedness and forgiveness. These are very attractive words, but at the same time, very testing words. They describe in detail what the Lord meant when He gave us a new commandment to love one another as He had loved us. It is through this love that people know we are His disciples (John 13:34-35).

The Holy Spirit describes love most poetically and powerfully in 1 Corinthians 13. The beauty of God's word always touches our hearts. But in doing so, it never loses the sharpness of a two-edged sword. You will not find more extraordinary poetry than 1 Corinthians 13, but you also find the most profound challenges to the expression of love in our lives:

> "Love suffers long and is kind; love does not envy; love does not parade itself, is not puffed up; does not behave rudely, does not seek its own, is not provoked, thinks no evil; does not rejoice in iniquity, but rejoices in the truth; bears all things, believes all things, hopes all things, endures all things. Love never fails" (1 Corinthians 13:4-8).

In these verses God has given us very beautiful and powerful statements against which to compare our love. And Paul gives us the highest reference point of all – the Lord Jesus. "Walk in love as Christ also loved us and gave Himself for us."

For a couple of years, whilst I worked on a project, I had to stay regularly in hotels close to Heathrow Airport in London. In the hotel rooms there was often a free copy of a business magazine. Inside, it listed the world's wealthiest people. In those days, Bill Gates was always at the top of that list. I think he was worth then around 50 billion dollars. But all the people on the list had one thing in common: their wealth could be measured. Paul writes in 2 Corinthians 8:9, "For you know the grace of our Lord Jesus Christ, that though He was rich, yet for your sakes He became poor, that you through His poverty might become rich." We can never measure the richness of Christ, nor do I believe we will ever know the depth of His poverty. But we know His grace and the love that led Him to give Himself for us.

God's love for the world is expressed in John 3:16 and in 1 John 3:16, John writes, "By this we know love, because He laid down His life for us." We imitate and walk in the love of Christ by laying "down our lives for the brethren." Then in verse 18, John challenges us as the children of God, "My little children, let us not love in word or in tongue, but in deed and in truth."

Day 88

Walk as children of light

For you were once darkness, but now you are light in the Lord. Walk as children of light (for the fruit of the Spirit [or, light] is in all goodness, righteousness, and truth). *(Ephesians 5:8-9)*

We once went as a family to the National Coal Mining Museum for England near Wakefield, Yorkshire. You are taken through the history of mining by men who used to be miners. To do this, you have a miner's helmet and lamp, and descend a deep mineshaft in a cage. At the bottom of the shaft, as we grouped, our guide told us to turn off our lights. And we stood in darkness that I will never forget. I put my hand to my face to look at it, but there was only an impenetrable blackness you could almost feel. It was a relief, even after a few moments, to turn the miner's lamp back on and for the darkness to disappear.

In Ephesians 5:8 Paul wasn't describing physical darkness but the moral and spiritual darkness his readers once inhabited and which had inhabited them. But then God's light shone into their hearts. They became "light in the Lord" and "the children of light". These phrases describe our spiritual position in Christ, our standing. But we also have the privilege and responsibility of walking as the children of light. In this way, we witness to our Lord and Saviour in a world that is still in moral and spiritual darkness. This walk describes our daily lives before God, our state. There is always the danger that we may not live in the way God intends us to live. To address this danger, Paul always encouraged the people of God to walk in good works, to walk worthy of their heavenly calling, to walk in love and to walk as children of light. The word for light is at the root of the word 'phosphorus' – "light-bearing".

Although our verse reads "the fruit of the Spirit", and the Holy Spirit is the power by which we live for Christ, the reading more generally held to be accurate is "the fruit of the light". Paul associates this fruit with all goodness, righteousness, and truth. Goodness expresses the goodness of God in the selfless actions of His children which benefit others. We are made righteous through faith in Christ. And our lives should be consistent with what we are in Christ. It is not self-righteousness but righteousness expressed by humbly seeking and obeying God's will. David writes about God leading him in paths of righteousness. In this righteousness, we act with integrity before God, towards each other and indeed all people.

Pilate said to Jesus, "What is truth?" but didn't wait for the answer. We live in a world that increasingly rejects absolutes. But we believe in the Lord Jesus Christ who is the way, the truth and the life. In John 17, Jesus also tells us that God's word is truth, and it sanctifies us. Through communion with Christ and obedience to the word of God, the reality of the life we have in Christ is seen.

In 2 Corinthians 4:6 we read, "For it is the God who commanded light to shine out of darkness, who has shone in our hearts to give the light of the knowledge of the glory of God in the face of Jesus Christ." Our daily response to this is found in Philippians 2:14-15, "Do all things without complaining and disputing, that you may become blameless and harmless, children of God without fault in the midst of a crooked and perverse generation, among whom you shine as lights in the world."

Day 89

A grain of wheat

Most assuredly, I say to you, unless a grain of wheat falls into the ground and dies, it remains alone; but if it dies, it produces much grain. (John 12:24)

I live in Lincolnshire. It is the second largest English county after Yorkshire and known for growing vast amounts of wheat and other cereals, as well as all kinds of vegetables. In my car I often pass fields of wheat swaying in the breeze. It would be difficult to count all the stalks of wheat, let alone the grains. Each grain is under 10mm long. You can easily sift one in your hands, as the disciples did when they were hungry while walking with the Lord.

The pictures we are given of our Saviour, Jesus Christ, are remarkable. Abraham sacrificed a ram in the place of Isaac his son, families sacrificed the Passover lambs for generations. Samuel sacrificed a suckling lamb for a nation. All these occasions looked forward to the time when John the Baptist would announce Jesus as the Lamb of God in the opening chapter of John's Gospel. In the same Gospel the Lord Jesus speaks of Himself as the Bread of Life (John 6:35), the Light of the world (John 8:12), the Door (John 10:7), the Good Shepherd (10:11), the Resurrection and the Life (John 11:25), the Way, the Truth and the Life (John 14:6) and as the true Vine (John 15:1). Each of these beautiful and powerful illustrations gives us an understanding of the majesty of the Person and of the work of the Lord Jesus, and bows our hearts in worship.

In John 12, six days before the Passover, those who loved Jesus at Bethany made him a supper, a reminder of what we do when we break bread. Mary worshipped Jesus by anointing His feet with precious oil, a lovely illustration of true worship from the hearts of those who form the Church of Christ. Shortly afterwards at Jerusalem, a large crowd took branches of palm trees and praised Jesus crying out,

> "Hosanna! 'Blessed is He who comes in the name of the Lord!' The King of Israel!" (John 12:13)

The Jewish people briefly worshipped their King. Then, a little later, a group of Greeks, who were in Jerusalem to worship at the feast, came to Philip and asked him, "Sir, we wish to see Jesus" (John 12:21), an illustration of Gentiles coming to Jesus at the end of His ministry, as the wise men did when Jesus was born.

Philip and Andrew told Jesus about the Greeks' request. And this was the moment when Jesus described Himself in the most incredible way – as a grain of wheat. Worship fills our hearts as we listen to the Lord Jesus describe His death and resurrection and all that it would bring about for the glory of God, using the analogy of a grain of wheat. Of all the pictures there is none so small, so simple in character or so isolated, when sown, as the grain of wheat. But none so vivid in its fruitfulness. The Lord of Glory felt in His soul both the weight and isolation of Calvary and His complete devotion to His Father. The Father responds from heaven and speaks of His glory in the Person of His Eternal Son throughout His peerless life and ultimately in His death and resurrection: "I have both glorified it and will glorify it again" (John 12:28).

As we remember the Lord Jesus, may worship continue to fill our hearts afresh as we consider John's record of how the Person who brought everything into being became like a grain of wheat in love for us.

Day 90

Monday 15 June 2020

Walk in wisdom

See then that you walk circumspectly, not as fools but as wise, redeeming the time, because the days are evil. (Ephesians 5:15-16)

I like words that are not in common use such as "circumspect". Understanding their usage enriches our appreciation of language. "Circumspect" comes from the Latin *circum* meaning "around" and *specere* meaning "to look". Literally, that conveys the idea of looking carefully and accurately at things. It is a feature of wisdom which, in its wider sense, does not take things at face value. It weighs them up and considers the potential consequences before making decisions and acting on them.

We live in a world that wants us to make quick decisions. That is why images are so important in marketing products. If people like the look of something, the overriding urge is to possess it. This can lead to poor judgements and unhappy and sometimes tragic consequences. In the opening chapters of the Bible, Eve "saw that the tree was good for food, that it was pleasant to the eyes, and a tree desirable to make one wise, she took of its fruit and ate" (Genesis 3:6). Later in Genesis, Lot "lifted his eyes and saw all the plain of Jordan, that it was well-watered everywhere (before the LORD destroyed Sodom and Gomorrah) like the garden of the LORD, like the land of Egypt as you go toward Zoar" (Genesis 13:10). Notice the connection in both passages with Eden. The garden of Eden was a place God provided so He could have fellowship with people. That fellowship was broken. People yearn for a materially perfect place but there is no spiritual desire or responsibility towards the Person who alone can meet our true need – salvation. Lot longed for Egypt, which in the Bible is a picture of the world, and it was a spiritual man who took him there – Abraham. Although Lot left Egypt, Egypt was still in his heart. If Abraham had walked circumspectly he would not have put himself, his wife and his nephew in physical, moral and spiritual danger. God delivered and blessed Abraham. But when Lot's decision-making was influenced by his experience of Egypt, there were tragic consequences.

The Lord Jesus told His disciples to be as wise as serpents and as harmless as doves. Grace makes us wise, not foolish. We live in a dangerous and evil world. You don't need to be a Christian to realise such is the case. It has been so encouraging to take advantage of video conferencing to maintain the fellowship and the encouragement of the people of God over recent months. We can also use the internet to witness in new ways. But the internet is also used to defraud, bully, blackmail and destroy people's relationships and lives. And it is further used to damage the infrastructure of economies and endanger the world's safety.

Billy Bray, the remarkable Cornish miner and Christian, was walking home from work late one evening. The path he took was dark and lonely, and his colleagues decided they would take the opportunity to frighten this man of God. So they hid in the trees and made strange noises; one called out, "Billy, it's Satan, I'm over here." Billy calmly replied, "You can't be Satan; you are too far away." Evil is never far away. The Lord Jesus wants us to be wise and consider carefully the small and great steps we take, and to understand the preciousness of time and how we can best use it. It is in His presence that we learn this wisdom that comes from above (James 3:17-18) and how to walk in it.

Day 91

Tuesday 16 June 2020

The power of intercession

Christ ... who also makes intercession for us.　　(Romans 8:34)

Many years ago, Mr Jack Packer, who ran the Sunday School which I went to, had a severe heart attack. In the Lord's goodness, he made a remarkable recovery and was eventually sent home. One day I went to a local park with my friend Paul to practice our rugby skills. On the way home, we had to pass the street where the Packers lived. The road we walked down was full of shops. I suddenly had the idea of buying Mr Packer some grapes and suggested this to Paul. He agreed. So we went into a fruit shop and bought some grapes. On reflection the grapes were definitely not from Eshcol and the brown paper bag did not add to their appeal, but on we pressed and arrived a few minutes later at Mr Packer's home. Mrs Packer answered the door, and we presented our gift in a bag which had become quite damp. Mrs Packer thanked us very much, and we went on our way. When Mr Packer had recovered, he and his dear wife invited Paul and me to their home every Thursday evening. Mr Packer taught us to play chess, and Mrs Packer introduced us to fruit juices and cakes we had never tasted before. For a long time, they devoted their Thursday evenings to show us the kindness they had learnt from their Saviour. I can never remember them preaching to us, but on many occasions the conversation touched on spiritual things.

This taught me how God can move, without the intervention of anyone else, in the mind of a young person to make a tiny decision which would result in his blessing. And how God can move His people to take opportunities to develop relationships and use their homes for the spiritual benefit of others.

At that time, people were praying for me. We should never underestimate the power of prayer. It is essential to intercede at the throne of grace to ask the Lord Jesus to intervene in people's lives. Over recent times we have felt our prayers were too general and imprecise. God wants us to be precise and transparent in our prayers. This is not because God doesn't know what our needs are, but because it makes us more compassionate. Compassion is feeling the needs of others in our hearts. It teaches us the feelings of Christ, our Great High Priest. Prayer brings us into the presence of God. There we understand our weakness and inability to change things, but find ourselves in the presence of the One who can. At the same time, there are occasions when God allows us to be overwhelmed by a deep need, and we are unable to express ourselves clearly. But these prayers are articulated by the Holy Spirit, "For we do not know what we should pray for as we ought, but the Spirit Himself makes intercession" (Romans 8:26). They become the clearest of prayers. And as the Holy Spirit intercedes while in us and with us on earth, in heaven "It is Christ who died, and furthermore is also risen, who is even at the right hand of God, who also makes intercession for us" (Romans 8:34). Through prayer we are in touch through the intercessory ministry of the Spirit of God and the Son of God with our Father in heaven, which assures us nothing shall be able to separate us from the love of God which is in Christ Jesus our Lord (read Romans 8:26-39). In this powerful atmosphere, our prayers are heard. It is a privilege we should never neglect.

Day 92

Wednesday 17 June 2020

Caleb

I am still as strong today as I was in the day that Moses sent me; my strength now is as my strength was then, for war and for going and coming. *(Joshua 14:11, ESV)*

Last evening I was speaking to an old friend who is in his ninetieth year. He lives alone, and I rang him as I wanted to know how he was getting on in lockdown, and to encourage him. I came off the telephone feeling so encouraged myself by a brother who was still so bright in his faith, positive in his outlook and with such a thankful spirit. He reminded me so much of Caleb.

Caleb must have felt so excited to be chosen as one of the twelve men sent by Moses to survey the land God had promised His people. The men travelled from the Negev to Hebron. When they returned, they said the land did indeed flow with milk and honey! And they showed the people the grapes of Eshcol, and the pomegranates and figs they had brought back. But then they said, "We are not able to go up against the people, for they are stronger than we are" (Numbers 13:31, ESV). How depressing to be shown what God had long promised, and then to be told you can't have it. Caleb had said, "Let us go up at once and take possession, for we are well able to overcome it" (Numbers 13:30). If ever there was a man of faith, it was Caleb. He believed God had led His people to the edge of the Promised Land; he had walked through it and seen it was precisely as God described, and he was ready to possess it straight away. God says of Caleb, "My servant Caleb, because he has a different spirit in him and has followed Me fully, I will bring into the land where he went, and his descendants shall inherit it" (Numbers 14:24). On three further occasions, Caleb is spoken of as following the Lord wholeheartedly (Numbers 32:12, Deuteronomy 1:36, Joshua 14:14).

Caleb was ready to fight giants to possess and enjoy what God had promised. It was Harold St. John who started an address on Ephesians with the words, "I am the owner of many umbrellas, but the possessor of few!" He was using this as a reminder of how we need to take hold of and possess what God has given us. The Children of Israel made the wilderness their home. Caleb's generation died there, having never seen the land God wanted them to have. What is so striking about Caleb is the faith, love and hope he already possessed. His faith never let his disappointment create frustration and bitterness in his heart. So often, when we are disappointed, we are robbed of joy and can become resentful. Instead, in love, Caleb suffered with the people of God as they wandered through the wilderness that was never his home. And all the time, hope shone brightly in his heart with the certainty that he would possess Hebron. Read his joyous story in Joshua 14 and how as an eighty-five-year-old man he said, "I am still as strong today as I was in the day that Moses sent me; my strength now is as my strength was then, for war and for going and coming. So now give me this hill country of which the Lord spoke on that day" (verses 11-12, ESV). These were not idle words. He met and defeated giants and possessed Hebron as his inheritance.

We face the giants of fear, doubt and weakness that can make us retreat to the safety of the wilderness and miss out on the spiritual blessings God wants us to enjoy and be empowered by. He gives examples like Caleb and saints like my dear old friend to encourage us to have a bright faith, to love in all circumstances and to be transformed by the hope we have in Christ.

Day 93

Thursday 18 June 2020

Promises leading to peace

"Peace I leave with you, My peace I give to you".　　　*(John 14:27)*

My mother-in-law used to say, "Your promises are like pie crusts – always breaking." I hasten to add this wasn't directed at me personally! I have often thought of how true these words can be. Keeping promises is a challenge and we often find out we are unable to deliver on our word.

In John 14 we discover Jesus Christ makes and keeps extra-ordinary promises. John is the only gospel writer to give us such a full account of the words and actions of Jesus on the Passover night before He was arrested and crucified. Even though the cross lay before Him, His words, contained in chapters 13 to 17, are not filled with sorrow and dismay. They are the most compelling descriptions of the Lord's love for us and His promises to us; promises He was able to keep. He begins by presenting Himself as the object of our faith: "Believe also in Me" (verse 1). He would no longer be the object of sight to a few faithful followers on earth, but the object of faith in heaven to the millions who would trust and follow Him. In verse 2 He promises a place prepared for us in heaven: "I go to prepare a place for you." The disciples had looked for an earthly kingdom, but Christ promised an inheritance in heaven. We are citizens of heaven, and the power to live on earth comes from our connection with Christ in heaven. The Lord Jesus promises, in verse 3, His personal return from heaven: "I will come again, and receive you to Myself." He promised to come again and personally take them into the Father's house in heaven. At the end of the same verse He promises His presence: "where I am, there you may be also." On the cross the Lord promised the dying, repentant thief he would be with Him in Paradise. In these few verses the Lord fixes our faith and hope in Himself in heaven. Christians can be vague about heaven. The Lord brings it into focus. It's about the Person. Just as we saw God's love, grace and power in Jesus on earth, so we know these features in our living and all-powerful Saviour in heaven.

This leads us to the here and now. In verse 13 the Lord introduces them to the power of praying in His name: "Whatever you ask in My name, that I will do." God's love for the world was seen at the cross. The name of Jesus was written over that cross. It is the same name that "is above every name" (Philippians 2:9). Jesus is both our Saviour and our Lord. As we came to Him for salvation, so we go to Him for everything, asking in His name. In verses 16-17 of our chapter the Lord Jesus promises the Holy Spirit as a helper: "I will pray the Father, and He will give you another Helper, that He may abide with you for ever, even the Spirit of truth." Jesus was not going to leave them as orphans. He was going to send another Helper; another Helper of the same kind. If we want to know who the Holy Spirit is like, then look at Jesus. He is in us, and He is with us. Finally, in verse 27, the Lord Jesus promises peace, "Peace I leave with you, My peace I give unto you; not as the world gives do I give to you. Let not your heart be troubled, neither let it be afraid." As the storm of Calvary came into sight, Jesus promised His disciples peace. He is the Prince of peace.

Christ's work is finished, our salvation is secure, and our destiny is assured. It is here and now we prove the reality of what we have in Christ. We do this by trusting the Saviour and walking with Him, being led and empowered by the Holy Spirit of God, and by being freed from anxiety to know the peace of God in every circumstance of life.

Day 94

Friday 19 June 2020

I am the way, the truth, and the life (1)

I am … (John 14:6)

Of all the "I am" statements of the Lord Jesus in John's gospel, "I am the way, the truth, and the life" is the most comprehensive. The Lord Jesus is the only way of salvation, the absolute truth and the One who gives and sustains life. We live in a world which has all but ceased to believe in absolutes. Everything is relative to how the individual feels and thinks. The Christian faith is based upon the absolute statements of the Son of God. Thomas was confused and told the Lord that the disciples did not know where He was going, so how could they know the way? Thomas, even as a disciple of Jesus, failed to understand the work of Christ but his question served to draw the answer that still bows our heart in worship: "I am the way, the truth, and the life. No one comes to the Father except through Me." In verse 8, Philip also failed to understand the Person of Christ when he asked Jesus, to show the disciples the Father. You sense the disappointment in the Lord's heart when He replied, "Have I been with you so long, and yet you have not known Me, Philip? He who has seen Me has seen the Father; so how can you say, 'Show us the Father'? Do you not believe that I am in the Father, and the Father in Me?" (verses 9-10).

It has always been difficult for people to understand how the lowly Jesus of Nazareth could be the way of salvation, the embodiment of truth, the One who is life and the perfect expression of God. That is why we need to consider the first two words of our verse, "I am", before exploring the meaning of the way, the truth and the life. These two tiny words link the Jesus of the New Testament to the Jehovah of the Old Testament. The God whom Israel worshipped was the Person who created everything. He was all-knowing and all-powerful. He revealed Himself to Moses in Exodus 3:14 as the "I am". It is interesting that in the same passage God speaks to Moses about His people. He saw their oppression in Egypt, heard their cry of suffering, knew their sorrows and as the "I am" He was going to come down and deliver them (Exodus 3:7-8). This theme runs powerfully through the whole of the Old Testament. God is presented as the only Saviour. His word is truth, and He is the Creator and upholder of life. But the "I am" was only known from a distance. Even Moses was not allowed to see Him in all His glory. The High Priest could only go into the Holy of Holies in the Tabernacle and the Temple on a special annual occasion. God's presence and His power to save was unquestioned, but there was always a distance between Him and His people.

The fullness of the heart of God and His true nature were never fully revealed until Jesus came into the world. We must always remember that the Person who came into creation was the Creator. It was God who became Man. It was the Son who became the Servant. John chapter 1 declares, "In the beginning was the Word, and the Word was with God, and the Word was God" (John 1:1). The deity of the Lord Jesus is presented throughout this gospel. It is John who records Jesus' words, "Before Abraham was, I am" (John 8:58). When the officers came to arrest Jesus of Nazareth, He replied, "I am He" and they drew back and fell to the ground (John 18:6).

The deity of Christ is fundamental to the Christian faith. Today it is questioned and denied with many other fundamentals of the Christian faith. How important it is that we assert the truth and live in the joy of knowing the One who, as He went in love to Calvary, said, "I am the way, the truth, and the life."

Day 95

Saturday 20 June 2020

I am the way, the truth, and the life (2)

I am the way ... (John 14:6)

If you came to my house, you would generally come in the front door. But you could also go through the back door or the patio door that opens onto the garden. In the Old Testament, the Tabernacle which God designed had only one entrance. There were no side or back ways into God's dwelling place. God was demonstrating to us that there is only one way into His presence. When we come to the New Testament, we learn that way is a Person, Jesus Christ.

The Old Testament promised God's Messiah. The Jews and even the Samaritans looked for Him. The woman at the well told Jesus she knew the Messiah was coming (John 4:25). A Saviour was expected. But Jesus was a surprise to His people. They understood the Messiah to be a mighty deliverer who would set them free from Rome and establish an earthly kingdom. Instead, the Lord Jesus revealed Himself as a far greater Saviour, not only dealing with the needs of His people in Israel, but the One who was "the Lamb of God who takes away the sin of the world" (John 1:29). God made it clear when sin entered the world that a sacrifice was needed to bring people to God. It was God who made the first sacrifice when He killed the animals to clothe Adam and Eve (Genesis 3:21). Abraham explained to Isaac that God would provide a lamb for a burnt offering (Genesis 22:8). When God instituted the Passover, He said when He saw the blood, He would pass over them (Exodus 12:13). All these pictures and types looked on to the Lord Jesus who "not with the blood of goats and calves, but with His own blood

... entered the Most Holy Place once for all, having obtained eternal redemption" (Hebrews 9:12). Now we have boldness "to enter the Holiest by the blood of Jesus" (Hebrews 10:19).

When the passenger ferry *Herald of Free Enterprise* sank outside the Belgian port of Zeebrugge in 1987, many people lost their lives. There were heroic stories of those who tried to save others. In one remarkable instance, a man made himself into a human bridge so that people could walk over him to safety. This is what the Lord Jesus did for the world; He became the way to God by the sacrifice of Himself. When we came to Christ, we knew with absolute clarity that Jesus was the only way to God. We trusted implicitly in the Lord Jesus, and the blessing of salvation filled our hearts.

But during our lives we often go our own way and struggle in our own strength. We are like a brother who was once travelling through Israel. He wanted to find the way to a particular place. He stopped a local man and asked him. The man said he would take him. But the brother said he only needed to know the way. The man replied, "I am the way." Now in resurrection and the power of an endless life, the Lord Jesus is still the way and He is able to save completely those who come to God through Him (Hebrews 7:25).

We don't merely need directions. We need the One who still says to our hearts, "I am the way" and who invites us to walk day-by-day with Him.

Day 96

Sunday 21 June 2020

We will remember your love

The Son of God, who loved me and gave Himself for me.

(Galatians 2:20)

Christ also loved the church and gave Himself for her.

(Ephesians 5:25)

It is a joy to sit with fellow Christians at the beginning of the week in the simple meeting we call the Lord's Supper. I think of the Saviour at the centre of heaven in all the power and glory of His resurrection. It is humbling to know that He looks down – into this world which rejected and crucified Him – to draw His people around Himself, with the love that fills His shepherd's heart.

When as children we played in the street with our friends after school, my mother would call us to tell us it was teatime. Soon we were all sat down to eat in a family where we were loved. Everything else was left outside. There was a time when the Lord Jesus was left outside. At the Passover, His disciples, so occupied with themselves, argued about who should be the greatest. Even Peter, James and John fell asleep when the Lord needed them to watch with Him in the Garden of Gethsemane. But at the Lord's Supper it is the world that is left outside. And Christ draws us together, in large companies or in the twos and threes, to know we are loved. Each of us is there because the Lord loved us individually. And, like Paul, we can say, "The Son of God who loved me and gave Himself for me" (Galatians 2:20). Our lives represent a unique expression of the love of Christ. Paul lived a remarkable life for God: the dying, repentant thief had no time to do anything other than believe in the Lord Jesus. These two saints and all the vast company of the redeemed will only be in heaven because Christ loved us and gave Himself for us. The Lord Jesus affirms His love for us and values the genuine expressions of gratitude and praise which rise from our hearts. Worship in the Bible is often expressed in silent adoration. At the beginning of the Lord's life on earth, the wise men, overwhelmed by the incarnation when they saw Immanuel, worshipped. Mary of Bethany, towards the end of the Lord's life on earth, was overwhelmed by the One who is the resurrection and the life, and worshipped. Their worship ascended to heaven, as does ours.

We also sit before the Lord Jesus as members of the Body of Christ, the Church. The Lord explains to us the depth of His love for His Church in a simple picture in Matthew: "Again, the kingdom of heaven is like a merchant seeking beautiful pearls, who, when he had found one pearl of great price, went and sold all that he had and bought it" (Matthew 13:45-46). The cost of our salvation was immense. Now what the Lord Jesus seeks is not perfect expressions or the sweetest, harmonious voices, but the genuine response of love rising from hearts joined together as one to remember and worship our Saviour. When the Lord Jesus gathered His disciples in an upper room over 2000 years ago, He did it with a deep desire (Luke 22:15) and endless love for His own (John 13:1). We should draw near to Him this morning with a deep desire, and love in our hearts, to respond to words the Saviour addresses to each of His sheep and to the one flock: "Remember Me."

Day 97

Monday 22 June 2020

I am the way, the truth, and the life (3)

I am the way, the truth ... (John14:6)

"What is truth?" was Pilate's question to Jesus in John 18:38. Interestingly, he did not wait for the answer. Not only great thinkers, but also the most ordinary of people, have asked the same question. Today, the fashion is to think that truth is no longer absolute, but open to interpretation depending upon how we feel or think. John 14:6 teaches us that truth is found in a Person – Jesus Christ. Jesus had told Pilate that He had to come into the world to bear witness to the truth and that everyone who is of the truth heard His voice. Truth has been described as the reality lying at the basis of an appearance – the essence of a matter. In Romans 15:8 we read about the "truth of God" and how God, in Christ, had fulfilled His promises. All the Old Testament promises and prophecies were centred on Christ. On the road to Emmaus, in Luke 24, Jesus went through the whole of the Old Testament expounding the things concerning Himself to the two disciples who were walking with Him. Later they spoke of their heart burning within them (Luke 24:32) as He opened the Scriptures, so they could understand. They were "of the truth and heard His voice" (John 18:37).

In Ephesians 4:21 we read that "the truth is in Jesus". This means that truth in all its fullness and scope is embodied in Him. He was the perfect expression of the truth. The Devil is described as having "no truth in him" and as a "liar and the father of lies" (John 8:44, ESV). He had deceived man from the very beginning of creation, and the consequences of that deception were catastrophic. Down the ages, God's truth had its effect in the lives of many of His people. However, despite all their faithfulness, failure was always present.

At the beginning of his Gospel, John describes the Lord Jesus as the Word – the manifestation of Deity: "And the Word became flesh and dwelt among us, and we beheld His glory, the glory as of the only begotten of the Father, full of grace and truth" (John 1:14). As the truth, all God's promises are summed up in His Son, the Lord Jesus Christ. His words, actions and thoughts were all perfect. In this world, the Lord Jesus showed us the truth of salvation, healing the sick and broken-hearted and bringing forgiveness. At Calvary, He displayed in the most profound way possible the truth of God's love. From the tomb, He showed the glorious truth of the resurrection. His ascension witnessed the reality of His glory. In glory, as the Head of the Church and our Great High Priest, He bears testimony to the truth of His constant love and care for His people. The One who has done all this will also return to bring us into the Father's house, establish His millennium kingdom, and fulfil all the purposes of God, that God may be all in all (1 Corinthians 15:28).

The Lord Jesus has brought us to know Him as the truth. He prayed that the Holy Spirit, the Spirit of Truth, would be with us and in us (John 14:17). He glorifies the Lord Jesus and empowers us to live for Him. And the Lord Jesus also prayed to the Father, "Sanctify them by Your truth. Your word is truth" (John 17:17), so that we would walk in holiness and witness to the One who is the way, the truth and the life.

Day 98

Tuesday 23 June 2020

I am the way, the truth, and the life (4)

I am the way, the truth, and the life. *(John 14:6)*

It is wonderful to realise that the Creator entered His creation. Billy Graham told the story of walking with his young son through some woods. They came across an anthill which had been partly destroyed. The ants were rushing about trying to repair their broken world. Billy Graham asked his son what he would like to do for the ants. The young boy replied, "I'd like to become an ant and help them repair their home."

When God looked down on His creation, so damaged by sin and its effects, His heart responded by sending His Son. When He came, He brought life (John 1:4). God spoke as the "I am" to Moses about redeeming His people (Exodus 3:8). I think God, in promising His people deliverance from slavery in Egypt, also looked on, in His mind and heart, to the time when Jesus would come down, as the Saviour of the world, to deliver.

In Luke 4:16, we read about Jesus coming to Nazareth, where He had been brought up (Luke 4:16). It is astonishing that Jesus, the Son of God, is referred to as being brought up in Nazareth. This was the place which Nathaniel doubted could produce any good thing (John 1:46). But it was in that lowly place that Jesus showed He was the life. In the synagogue on the Sabbath day He read from the book of Isaiah:

> "The Spirit of the Lord is upon Me,
> Because He has anointed Me
> To preach the Gospel to the poor;
> He has sent Me to heal the broken-hearted,

To proclaim liberty to the captives,
And recovery of sight to the blind,
To set at liberty those who are oppressed,
To proclaim the acceptable year of the Lord"
(Luke 4:18-19).

At last, the One who was the life was here and demonstrated its power. When He touched the leper, he was clean (Luke 5:13). When He spoke to the sea, it was calm (Luke 8:24). When He cast the demons out, there was peace (Luke 8:35). When He gave thanks for the five loaves and two fishes, thousands of people were fed (Luke 9:17). When He called to Lazarus in the tomb, he came out alive (John 11:44). Wherever Jesus went, He brought life (John 1:4).

The Lord Jesus said of His life, "I have power to lay it down and power to take it again" (John 10:18). God is light and God is love. The nature of God was manifested in the light of the life of Christ and in the love in which His life was laid down. But the Lord Jesus had power to take it again. In resurrection, we see life in all its victorious power. The book of Hebrews reminds us that Christ lives now for us in the power of an endless life (Hebrews 7:16). We share in that eternal life. "He who hears My words and believes in Him who sent Me has everlasting life, and shall not come into judgement but is passed from death into life" (John 5:24).

This life is to be expressed (1 John 2:6). The Lord Jesus lived for His Father when He was on earth. Now Christians are to live like Him on earth: "You were bought with a price; therefore glorify God in your body" (1 Corinthians 6:20). How do we glorify God? By living like the Lord Jesus did until the day when we shall live with Him.

Day 99

Wednesday 24 June 2020

The Body of Christ: Spiritual gifts

There are diversities of gifts, but the same Spirit.

(1 Corinthians 12:4, see verses 1-6)

The human body has a head, and lots of other external and internal parts. For the body to work correctly these different parts all connect to the brain. The nervous system provides this connection by which the brain sends its messages throughout the body, enabling us to express life. In 1 Corinthians 12 Paul uses the human body as an illustration of how the body of Christ works. The body of Christ embraces every true believer in the Lord Jesus Christ throughout the world. Its Head is in heaven – the Lord Jesus. Every member of the body has a function to perform, which helps the whole body to work properly and express the life of Christ. The Holy Spirit provides the connection between every member on earth and the Lord Jesus Christ in heaven.

The opening verse of the chapter is very interesting. Paul did not want the believers at Corinth to be uninformed. Christians can act in ways which show they are unaware of or disobedient to God's will. The Corinthian church, despite all its knowledge and gift, was divided, proud, worldly, and tolerated immorality. Paul wrote to them to put right the things which were wrong in their personal lives and in the church. One of the things they misunderstood was the use of spiritual gifts. The Corinthians' background was one of idolatry. Paul explains in 1 Corinthians 12:3 that Jesus is Lord and can only be recognised as such by the Holy Spirit. In the world, Christ is rejected; the Christian knows Him as Lord through the indwelling of the Spirit of God. It was typical for hostile Jews and heathens to exclaim "Anathema Jesus" – "Curse on Jesus". Paul reminded the Corinthians that it is the work of the Spirit of God to proclaim Jesus as Lord. The Lordship of Christ is the starting point of what Paul goes on to explain. Because Jesus is Lord, all that is done by Christians comes under His Lordship. As the brain guides and protects the body, so the Lord Jesus directs and builds His church by the power of the Spirit of God.

Paul also introduces the Trinity into the directing of spiritual gifts in verses 4-6. He explains that we do not all have the same gifts. However, when we use these different gifts under the direction of the Holy Spirit, they combine to benefit the whole body of Christ. First, it is the Holy Spirit who distributes various gifts. Verse 11 emphasises this: "The same Spirit works all these things, distributing to each one individually as He wills." Spiritual gifts can only be used effectively in the Spirit's power. It is the Lord Jesus who gives us different services to be undertaken for His glory. Spiritual gifts can only be used effectively under the Lord's authority. Finally, it is God who works in us to accomplish His will. Spiritual gifts can only be used effectively in God's will.

It is not by accident that Paul first describes the unity of the Godhead in connection with the distribution of spiritual gifts before he goes on to explain the unity of the body of Christ. By seeing the united purpose and action of the Godhead, we are encouraged to be united in purpose and action for the glory of God. One of the greatest dishonours to Christ is that His people are divided. His heartfelt prayer in John 17:11 was that "they may be one as We are". Paul demonstrates how this happens under the direction of the Godhead.

Day 100

Thursday 25 June 2020

The Body of Christ: The same Spirit

But the manifestation of the Spirit is given to each one for the profit of all. (1 *Corinthians 12:7, see verses 7-11*)

In 1 Corinthians 12:7 Paul explains an important principle. The manifestation of the Spirit through spiritual gifts is for the profit of the church. Sometimes, spiritual gifts can be regarded as a personal thing, to be used as we think fit. The Corinthians had become proud of their gifts and used them for self-glorification. The point of a gift is that it is given. It is not something which has its source in us but which has been given to us, in grace, by God. It is not to be used to draw attention to ourselves, but to build up Christ's Church. In using them, we are to act selflessly, not selfishly, and always seek to glorify the Lord Jesus and benefit His people.

In verses 8-10 Paul lists some of the spiritual gifts and links them to the work of the Holy Spirit. Spiritual gifts are also highlighted in other Scriptures: in Romans 12:6-8 they are related to the will of God; in Ephesians 4:10-16 they are given by the victorious, ascended Christ. In these passages we see the Godhead's provision for the welfare and blessing of the Church of Christ.

Today, the key thought is the Holy Spirit's giving. He gives in such a comprehensive and liberal way. The Father gave the Son, and the Son gave Himself. Now the Spirit gives, so freely, wisdom, knowledge, faith, healing, miracles, prophecy, discernment, tongues and interpretation. There is such a richness and diversity in His giving. God's glory in creation is seen in its wholeness and diversity. God's glory in His Church is seen in the same way through the same Spirit.

When the Lord returned to heaven, and the disciples watched Him taken up in glory, the angels spoke to them: "Men of Galilee, why do you stand gazing up into heaven? This same Jesus, who was taken up from you into heaven, will so come in like manner as you saw Him go into heaven" (Acts 1:11). It impressed me recently that the Lord Jesus never said goodbye. He said, "And I will pray the Father, and He will give you another Helper, that He may abide with you for ever, even the Spirit of truth, Whom the world cannot receive, because it neither sees Him nor knows Him; but you know Him, for He dwells with you and will be in you. I will not leave you orphans; I will come to you" (John 14:16-18).

Paul uses that lovely expression "the same Spirit" four times in verses 8-11. It is not just that He is the consistent power, but He is the Person in the Godhead working to glorify the Lord Jesus, worship the Father and bless us. He ceaselessly works in our hearts, resisting the flesh and moving our spirits to be more like Christ. And He gives each of us spiritual gifts. Mary of Bethany had a gift, and she sacrificed it in worship to the Saviour. In doing so, she blessed those who surrounded the Lord. The Holy Spirit gives us spiritual gifts. They are to be presented to Christ and used for the blessing of His Church. May God pour His grace into our hearts to use the spiritual gifts He has given us, to honour the Lord Jesus and to serve each other selflessly in love.

Day 101

Friday 26 June 2020

The Body of Christ: Many members

For as the body is one and has many members.

(1 Corinthians 12:12, see verses 12-17)

Paul continues to use the human body as an illustration of how the body of Christ functions. In 1 Corinthians 12:13 he reminds us of how we came into the body of Christ and how we are sustained within it. It is by the power of one Spirit that we have been baptised into one body. I became a member of the body of Christ when I trusted Christ through the work of the Spirit of God. Once saved, I am sustained in my new life by the ministry of the Holy Spirit. I need His ministry to enable me to enjoy and express my life in Christ in fellowship with other members of the Body of Christ. The Holy Spirit is in us all and with us all. He demonstrates His presence by building up each member and the whole Body of Christ.

There is an old Jewish fable about heaven and hell. In it, hell has a big table filled with the most appetising foods. Around the table are famished people who all have long spoons attached to their hands. The spoons are so long that it is impossible to get food to their mouths. Because they cannot feed themselves, they starve. In heaven, there is a similar table with the same kinds of delicious food. The people there also have long spoons attached to their hands. But they are all happy, well-fed and enjoying each other's company. Instead of trying to feed themselves, they used the long spoons to feed each other! The Spirit's work is to make us Christ-centred. This work puts the welfare of our fellow Christians at the centre of our thoughts. It also spills over into a concern for the spiritual blessing of other people.

In verses 15-16 the apostle explains what happens if I become self-centred and self-pitying. It is unfortunate when Christians become obsessed about what they are not. It may appear humble to think I am not useful because I am not gifted in the same way as another Christian. But it is not. It is a form of arrogance. I am really saying, God got it wrong because He did not make me like that brother or sister. I am also saying that I am not satisfied with God's will and purpose for me. There is also the further danger that, because we do not value God's purpose for us, we will not appreciate God's work in the lives of others. Such dissatisfaction is destructive, not constructive. In verse 15 Paul raises the question, "What would happen if the foot and ear decided to stop functioning because they were not a hand or an eye?" It would result in the whole body being disadvantaged. There are many functions to be fulfilled in the church, and each member is essential. Christ's church suffers when I am not prepared to be content with what God wants me to be.

The building we used, when I was a young Christian, had big and heavy mahogany benches. These had to be moved twice every Sunday for our different meetings. It was simple but heavy work. To do it, two brothers worked in harmony to move each bench. No one asked me to join in; it just seemed natural for me to help. It was my first experience of Christian service. I did it in fellowship with gifted brethren who were still prepared to do the simplest tasks. When we willingly fulfil what Christ has enabled us to do, we discover God supplies more grace and increases our usefulness, and the Body of Christ benefits. "Do not neglect the gift that is in you" (1 Timothy 4:14).

Day 102

Saturday 27 June 2020

The Body of Christ: God places the members

But now God has set the members, each one of them, in the body just as He pleased. (*1 Corinthians 12:18, see verses 18-20*)

In the Old Testament book of Exodus, Aaron the High Priest had a breastplate which he wore when he went into the presence of God. On it were twelve precious stones, arranged in rows. Jewellers have remarked that these stones were perfectly arranged not just to reflect the beauty of each stone, but to give out the combined radiance resulting from the way the stones were placed together. We are specially prepared by God to fill a unique role in His church, a place no one else can fill. We should not challenge the wisdom of God, but fulfil the ministry He has given us to do. 1 Corinthians 12:18 says, "God has set the members, each one of them, in the body just as He pleased." My father-in-law used to tell me, "Gordon, God has not put people in the church to please you, but to please Himself!" This helped me see the value God has placed on my brothers and sisters in Christ, and it encouraged me to value them more.

If we were all alike, the church would not be a body but a uniform mass. Sadly, soon after the church was formed, Christians began dividing into groups. Paul addresses such divisions in 1 Corinthians 1:10-13. Christians have repeated this behaviour down the ages thinking uniformity is unity. They have divided into groups to meet solely with Christians who think in exactly the same way. Artificial barriers have been created based on interpretation of the scriptures. Rules have been invented, and the dynamic experience of Christian fellowship lost. The benefit of each other's gifts and each other's presence is diluted. And the constant and necessary challenge to be Christ-like to maintain the unity of the Spirit, is sacrificed. How many Christians have left a fellowship just because they did not get on with other believers? Many use the highest principles to justify their position. But the church is robbed of fulfilling Christ's great desire as He went to the cross, "That they … may be one, as You, Father, are in Me, and I in You; that they also may be one in Us, that the world may believe that You sent Me" (John 17:21). It was a desire that our unity would make us witnesses to the love of God revealed in the Son of God.

Some Christian friends of mine who belong to a well-known Christian organisation once told me that they had the greatest experience of the body of Christ when they went away for a weekend with other members of the same organisation. Although they were from different backgrounds and fellowships, they could express unity. I had to say that, that although I was sure it was a happy experience, it was not what Christ had in mind. It is relatively easy to express fellowship with Christians we hardly know over a brief weekend together. It is far harder, and much more important, to witness to the body of Christ week in, week out with Christians you know very well and with whom you have to live and work. When, in those circumstances, we express the unity of Christ's church, it benefits the body and it leads people to Christ. When it does not happen, the people of God suffer, and people in the world are confused and sometimes driven away from Christ. Let us see Christ in one another and value and encourage the fellowship and gifts of fellow believers. And, through our fellowship, witness to the wonder of being in the body of Christ.

Day 103

Sunday 28 June 2020

The Body of Christ: Every Christian is needed

And the eye cannot say to the hand, "I have not need of you".
(1 Corinthians 12:21, see verses 21-26)

In 1 Corinthians 12:20 Paul reaffirms that the body has many members, and each one is needed! In the previous verses the problem was members of the body feeling they were not as gifted as they wanted to be. In verse 21 Paul turns to another issue – members of the body feeling superior to fellow Christians and not valuing them. He highlights self-centredness and independence. The comparisons he makes are interesting. The eye, with which we see, is compared to the hand with which we do things. The head, where the brain does the thinking, is compared to the feet which do the walking. He compares what represents perception, thoughtfulness and intelligence with what represents action, practicality and toughness. This point would not have been lost on the gifted but proud Corinthians. They liked the intellectual aspects of Christianity but had forgotten about the practical expression of true Christian love, which Paul brings home to them so beautifully and powerfully in chapter 13. God knows just what we are like. He knows that we can gravitate into particular groups and can begin to feel more important than other believers who do not think in precisely the same way as we do. And we can act in the most unchristian ways to support this behaviour. The eye and the head are higher up the body than the hands and the feet. But we would not get very far without these lower parts of the body. Paul teaches us that the members we can think are of little importance are essential to the body of Christ.

Paul points out that we dress physically to care for the whole body. It would be very unusual if we went out in the morning with an overcoat on but no shoes. We should not undervalue or exclude fellow believers for whom Christ died, but make every effort to acknowledge the value and contribution each one makes. This is so there are no divisions in the body and every member expresses the same care for every other member (verse 25).

When, for example, you injure your leg and it swells up, and it is difficult to move, what is happening? The body is coming to the aid of the damaged part by protecting it and immediately starting the healing process. Paul writes in verse 26, "If one member suffers all the members suffer with it." When we are ill, our whole body feels it and sympathises. That is how we are to react in the body of Christ. If one believer suffers, we are to act with compassion to protect them and encourage the healing that is needed. In so sympathising, we minister Christ, our great High Priest. He feels our needs and acts to meet them (Hebrews 4:14-16).

Equally, being in the church of Christ is a joyful experience. We should rejoice in the progress and expression of Christ seen in the lives of fellow Christians. It is an enormous encouragement to a brother or sister to know they are appreciated. We need to see Christ in one another and value our fellow believers, especially those with whom we meet regularly. In doing so, we not only demonstrate the One Body, we also reflect our Saviour who treasures each and every one of His people.

Day 104

The Body of Christ: God's gifts for the Church

And God has appointed these in the Church: first apostles, second prophets, third teachers …   (1 Corinthians 12:28, see verses 27-31)

In the final section of 1 Corinthians 12 Paul re-emphasises that the gatherings of God's people are part of the Body of Christ and we are individually members of it. God appoints and equips those who build up the Church. The gifts in verse 28 have an order. We also need to understand that some were for a specific period. Ephesians 2:20 explains that the Church is "built on the foundation of the apostles and prophets, Jesus Christ Himself being the chief cornerstone." After Christ's ascension, the apostles and prophets had the ministry of unfolding the revelation of God, which is now contained in the New Testament. The Lord Jesus told the apostles that the Holy Spirit of God would lead them into "all truth" (John 16:13). This ministry was completed in the first century of the Church's history. People cannot claim today to be Christ's apostles and prophets, because that work has been finished. In the list we are looking at, the apostles are placed first and prophets second. Teachers are placed third. Their ministry is to unfold all the Scriptures to the people of God and to be a living example of what they teach.

Evangelists are not mentioned, because Paul is stressing the building up of those who are already saved. He lists miracles, healing, helps, governments and tongues. Some of these gifts, such as miracles and healing, were confined to the apostolic period. This doesn't mean God does not still do the miraculous, but these were foundational gifts. Confined periods of miracles are seen in the ministry of Moses, Elijah and Elisha in the Old Testament, and that of the Lord Jesus and the apostles in the New Testament. Paul in later life was unable to heal some of his friends or himself. The gifts of being a help and support and giving spiritual guidance in the Church are still very much needed. These gifts should not be overlooked or undervalued. The gift of tongues was a sign, especially to unbelieving Jews, as Paul points out in 1 Corinthians 14:20-22.

Paul asks in verses 29-30 if we all have these gifts. No, we do not. They are shared, and he was about to show them, in chapter 13, a more excellent way, that of love. The Corinthians were indeed gifted people. But they had become disorderly, extravagant and self-centred in the way their gifts were used. Paul teaches us that we need the gifts God has given, but we are to use them in sacrificial service for the benefit and blessing of the flock of God. We are not to desire the gifts of others, but minister the gift God has given us in joyful and faithful service to the Lord Jesus. In the parable of the talents in Matthew 25:20 we get a lovely picture of a true servant, "Lord, you delivered to me five talents; look, I have gained five more talents besides them." It was a real joy for the servant to use what his lord had given him, and to present it to him.

I came home from work one day, when my daughter, Anna, was a young schoolgirl. The table was set for tea and on my side plate was a very unusual piece of rock-solid pastry. I asked Anna what it was, and with a smiling face, she replied, "I made it for you." Imperfection will always mark our service. But what the Lord rejoices in is the response of love for Him and His people. It is this love that Paul was about to bring before the hearts of the failing Corinthian church. It was the "more excellent way".

Day 105

Tuesday 30 June 2020

A stone's throw

And He was withdrawn from them about a stone's throw, and He knelt down and prayed, saying, "Father, if it is Your will, take this cup away from Me; nevertheless not My will, but Yours, be done."
(Luke 22:41-42)

The Spirit of God led Luke to mention the short distance the Lord Jesus placed between Himself and His disciples in the Garden of Gethsemane – a stone's throw. As the Lord prayed, He was in sight of His disciples. He asked Peter, James and John to watch with Him as He felt in His heart the weight of Calvary. A little later, an angel would come to strengthen Him. C.A. Coates' hymn brings before our souls the Good Shepherd who was about to die for His sheep:

> Thy grace, O Lord, that measured once the deep
>   Of Calvary's woe, to seek and save Thy sheep,
> Has touched our hearts and made them long for Thee,
>   Thyself our treasure and our all to be.

The Garden of Eden teaches us about the rejection of God's will. For thousands of years the consequences of that decision had afflicted the world. In Luke 4, in the first words of His public ministry, Jesus described a world filled with the poor, the broken-hearted, the enslaved, the blind and the oppressed. It is a world that has not changed. The words of Jesus measured the distance people were from God. Kneeling down in Gethsemane, the Lord Jesus measured the cost of our redemption.

Before David entered the Valley of Elah, he had killed the lion and the bear. Before Jesus went to Calvary, He had destroyed the works of the devil. He had healed, set free, opened eyes, forgiven and brought peace. But these beautiful works could not save the world. He had to take the cup which the Father had given Him. At the Lord's supper, we remember the Saviour's love that took Him down into the 'valley' that was Calvary.

David went to meet Goliath from his father's flock, dressed as a shepherd, but in all the power of the God of Israel. The Saviour rises from the Father's presence, not in weakness but in all the power of divine love, to say, "Shall I not drink the cup which My Father has given Me?" (John 18:11).

We have been longing for lockdown restrictions to be lifted, and looking forward to being able to enjoy normal Christian fellowship again. The steps towards this are being carefully considered. We have so much missed being able to sing together. As we remember the Lord Jesus next Lord's Day, may a song rise from our hearts that goes beyond any physical restrictions placed on us, to tell the Lord we are filled with gratitude for His redeeming love. He measured the distance we were from God. He measured the cost of removing that distance. He gave Himself for us. Now there is not a stone's throw distance between the Lord and us. We are in Christ. We cannot be nearer. And nothing can prevent the new song He has put in our hearts being heard in joy by Him.

About the Author

Gordon Kell has been involved in Christian ministry for over fifty years. Apart from a period of five years in full-time Christian service, this has always been in a "tentmaking" capacity. With his wife, June, their Christian ministry has included young peoples' work, camps, Christian holidays, young married couples' weekends, and conferences throughout the UK and occasionally in Europe. Until recently, Gordon's written ministry was linked with his long involvement in radio Bible teaching. Gordon and June have one daughter, three granddaughters and a grandson, and live in Northern Lincolnshire, not far from the birthplace of John Wesley who once said, "Let your words be the genuine picture of your heart."

Gordon commands a wide respect for "rightly handling the word of truth" (2 Timothy 2:15), combining awareness of its depth with succinctness and a personable style.